Date Due

Shut-in.			
BC482			
VANlan88			
Zurich			
OCT 18 1988			
JAN 25 1990			
MAY 2 8 199			
FEB 1 7 2001			
FEB 2 0 2001			
NOV 13 2001			

LIFE IN UPPER CANADA

LIFE IN
UPPER CANADA

WESLEY B. TURNER

FOCUS ON CANADIAN HISTORY SERIES

GROLIER LIMITED/TORONTO

To my family

Cover: King St. East, Toronto, 1835

Cover design: Didier Fiszel

Maps: Tibor Kovalik

Selected Further Reading courtesy Maureen Kaukinen, East York Board of Education

Illustration Credits: Metropolitan Toronto Library Board, cover and pages 14, 16, 22, 25, 36, 39, 61, 64, 69, 72, 80, 84, 85, 86; Ontario Archives, page 17; Public Archives of Canada, pages 26, 66; Metropolitan Toronto & Region Conservation Authority, Black Creek Pioneer Village, pages 28, 45, 46, 47, 49, 51, 52, 53, 54, 56, 58, 70, 75, 76, 77, 83; Macmillan Company of Canada, page 43; Confederation Life Association, page 68; Dundurn Castle, Hamilton Historical Board, page 71; Kingston Whig-Standard, page 79.

Canadian Cataloguing in Publication Data

Turner, Wesley B., 1933-
Life in Upper Canada

(Focus on Canadian history series)

Includes index.
ISBN 0-7172-1802-3

1. Ontario — History — 1791-1841.* 2. Frontier and pioneer life — Ontario. I. Title. II. Series.

FC3071.T87	971.3'02	C79-094923-7
F1058.T87		

Printed and Bound in Canada

Contents

Preface   7

Introduction   9

New Settlers Create a Province   11

The People of Upper Canada   21

Life on a Pioneer Farm   42

Life in the Towns and Cities   60

The Growth of Upper Canada   74

Selected Biographies   88

For Discussion   92

Selected Further Reading   95

Index   96

Preface

Have you ever wondered what pioneer life in Ontario was like? What kind of house would you live in? What clothes would you wear? What food would you eat? What games would you play? What work would you do at home and in school? You will find some of the answers in a study of social history. The past can be examined in a variety of ways, for example, through political history, economic history or historical geography. But it is social history that concentrates on answering the sorts of questions raised above. When you know more about the past of your society, you will understand more about yourself and your family.

In other words, the past lives in the present. It lives not only in what you do but also in why you do certain things in certain ways. To take just one example, you do not attend school during the summer months because in earlier times, that was when children were needed to help on the farm.

You may like to visit old houses and towns, lumber camps and mines, and long-established farmsteads. You will find the pleasure of exploring these places is greatly increased when you know something of the people who made these and lived and worked in them. More and more we are trying to preserve what earlier men and women created. But to know what to preserve, and why, requires knowledge of the past.

There are many new and exciting books and articles on Upper Canada's history. These have provided me with ideas and arguments which I have tried to combine with the results of my own research and observation and present in brief and interesting form. I have enjoyed writing this book. Part of the reason is my association with Ken Pearson and the editors at Grolier who provided advice and encouragement. Most of all I appreciate the patience of my family. Of course, I accept the responsibility for whatever faults have escaped the editors' scrutiny.

Introduction

If you have you ever moved, you know what a big upheaval it is for a family to gather up its things and leave one place to go to another, even if the family stays in Canada and does not have to adjust to a new way of life. Yet we, today, can at least take all our personal and household belongings with us. We have moving companies to pack them up and transport them, and we nearly always have a house all ready to move into. And if we move, it is usually because someone in our own family decided that it will benefit us economically or that the city to which we are going will be a pleasanter place to live in. Things were very different for the people who came to Upper Canada in the late eighteenth and early nineteenth centuries.

This was particularly true in the case of the group chiefly responsible for the early settlement of Upper Canada, the United Empire Loyalists. They had to give up a great deal that was dear to them. They had lost their homes and land because they were loyal to the British during the American War of Independence. They did not really want to move. When they were obliged to do so, they did not even know for sure where they would go. Certainly they did not better themselves by going. Many of them were moving from a warmer and pleasanter climate to a colder and harsher one; they were leaving homes they had built for a piece of land which they would have to clear, where they would have to begin all over again putting up shelter and deciding which crops to grow.

Most of the settlers who followed the Loyalists to Upper

Canada did expect to better themselves by moving. But they still had the same problems to face — and frequently, even greater ones. Some did not speak English; many were city-dwellers or retired soldiers whose past life, however hard it might have been, had ill-prepared them for the particular kind of hardships pioneering involved.

Who were they and where did they come from? What various reasons caused them to leave everything they knew and take their chances in a wild and empty land? How did they manage, and what was life like for them in the pioneer society of Upper Canada?

Certainly, they changed the world they came to, but just as certainly it changed them too. How it all came about is one of the most fascinating aspects of the history of our country.

New Settlers Create a Province

Upper Canada, as such, was created in 1791, but its history began many years before that. It began with the colony of Quebec, which stretched from the Gulf of St. Lawrence beyond Lakes Huron and Erie. How was Upper Canada created, and why?

After the British took control of Quebec in 1760, the colony was ruled from Quebec City by an appointed governor and council, chosen by the British government. The governor received orders from Britain and, with the help of his council, carried them out in the best interests of the people of the colony. Otherwise, Quebec continued to follow French law as it had before the conquest. This arrangement left most things much as they had always been for the French in Quebec.

In the late 1770s and early 1780s, the arrival of the United Empire Loyalists, who settled along the St. Lawrence River west of Montreal, had a noticeable effect on the character of French Quebec. These newcomers did not speak French and for the most part were not Roman Catholics as were most of the French Canadians. Differences of language and religion were not the only ones, however, for the Loyalists were used to a different style of government and a different form of land ownership as well.

Because they had been forced from their land in the United States, the thing they wanted most was to own their own property. According to the law of Quebec, a person did not completely own his land: he was forced to pay dues to an overlord or *seignior*. The *seigniorial system* was very different from the British system of *freehold tenure*, under which a landowner owed nothing to an overlord.

Also, the Loyalists objected to being ruled completely by an appointed governor and council; they wanted a representative government, that is one which would have an assembly elected by the people to represent them.

Thus, while the French were reasonably content with the existing system of government and land ownership, the Loyalists were eager for change. The solution was to divide Quebec. In 1791, the British government passed the Constitutional or Canada Act, which created Upper and Lower Canada. Lower Canada was the area down the St. Lawrence River (that is, towards its mouth) where almost all the French-speaking people of Canada lived. Upper Canada was up the St. Lawrence River, west of Montreal. This division of Upper and Lower Canada lasted until the Union Act of 1841.

Under the Constitutional Act, a lieutenant governor was appointed for each province and an Executive Council was appointed to help him in his task of putting laws into effect. A legislature, or law-making body, was created, composed of a Legislative Council, also appointed, and a Legislative Assembly. The members of the Assembly were elected by adult males who owned a certain amount of land. The Assembly had the power to impose taxes within its province and make laws to serve local needs. The Legislative Council was also able to make laws and to approve — or disapprove — those laws passed by the Assembly.

The Act also allowed Upper Canada to have the kind of laws and land system the Loyalists were used to. Thus the Loyalists now had the two things they wanted: an elected Assembly and the right to own land.

The Assembly in Action — Politics and Rebellion

For many years, the government of Upper Canada worked fairly well. There were, of course, disagreements between appointed officials and elected officials, and two basic political groups

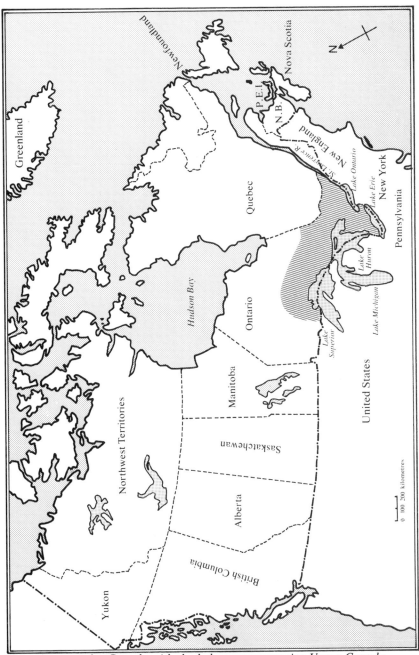

Map of present-day Canada with shaded area representing Upper Canada, 1791–1841.

John Graves Simcoe was appointed Upper Canada's first lieutenant governor in 1791.

gradually developed: the conservatives and the reformers.

Political conservatives wanted things to stay the way they were, or to change very slowly. They wanted the appointed officials — the lieutenant governor and the Executive and Legislative Councils — to be stronger than the elected Assembly. The reformers, on the other hand, believed that the Assembly, because it was elected by the people and represented them, should be the strongest part of the government.

Why did it make a difference which part of the government, the appointed or the elected, was stronger? In a general way, the appointed officials tended to look out for the interests of a small and relatively wealthy section of the society. The elected members of the Assembly, since they were voted in — and therefore could be thrown out — by the general population, were more likely to defend the interests of the ordinary settlers.

The conservatives believed that the Executive, that is, the lieutenant governor and the Executive Council, should be able to raise and spend money without interference from the Assembly and to give people jobs, or dismiss them, as they wished. This is called *patronage*. According to them, control of education, granting of land, and financial support of the Church of England, or Anglican Church, should all be in the hands of the appointed Executive. Many conservatives feared that a more democratic system would give people like farmers and laborers too much power.

The reformers wanted the Assembly to control government money, jobs, and land grants. Many did not want the government to support any church at all. They wanted the lieutenant governor, who was appointed by the British government, to listen to the Assembly and take its advice. All in all, the reformers wanted to lessen the power held by the small, wealthy ruling group and give more power to ordinary people. While most reformers wanted Canada to remain under British rule, they thought there were aspects of the American form of government that were valuable and should be part of their political system. They believed that the British system could be adjusted to their needs. The reformers included two groups — the moderates and the radicals. The moderates occasionally agreed with the conservatives on certain issues, but the radicals never did.

The best known radical was William Lyon Mackenzie. Mackenzie was very critical of the government. In a political journal which he founded — the *Colonial Advocate* — he attacked the group of people who really controlled the government. This group was called the *Family Compact*.

Mackenzie maintained that this small group was connected by family, marriage, and other ties. He complained that it controlled most of the government offices and benefited more than others from land grants and from such institutions as the Bank of Upper Canada, the Welland Canal Company, and the Canada Company. In short, the Family Compact ran Upper Canada for its own benefit at the expense of the people. The Family Compact dominated the Executive and Legislative Councils of Upper Canada until 1837. Its leader was John Strachan.

In 1837, Mackenzie, who was convinced that change would

PROCLAMATION

BY WILLIAM LYON MACKENZIE,

Chairman pro. tem. of the Provincial Government of the State of Upper Canada.

INHABITANTS OF UPPER CANADA!

For nearly fifty years has our country languished under the blighting influence of military despots, strangers from Europe, ruling us, not according to laws of our choice, but by the capricious dictates of their arbitrary power.

They have taxed us at their pleasure, robbed our exchequer, and carried off the proceeds to other lands—they have bribed and corrupted ministers of the Gospel, with the wealth raised by our industry—they have, in place of religious liberty, given rectories and clergy reserves to a foreign priesthood, with spiritual power dangerous to our peace as a people—they have bestowed millions of our lands on a company of Europeans for a nominal consideration, and left them to fleece and impoverish our country—they have spurned our petitions, involved us in their wars, excited feelings of national and sectional animosity in counties, townships and neighbourhoods, and ruled us, as Ireland has been ruled, to the advantage of persons in other lands, and to the prostration of our energies as a people.

We are wearied of these oppressions, and resolved to throw off the yoke. Rise, Canadians, rise as one man, and the glorious object of our wishes is accomplished.

Our intentions have been clearly stated to the world in the Declaration of Independence, adopted at Toronto on the 31st of July last, printed in the Constitution, Correspondent and Advocate, and the Liberal, which important paper was drawn by Dr. John Rolph and myself, signed by the Central Committee, received the sanction of a large majority of the people of the Province, west of Port Hope and Cobourg, and is well known to be in accordance with the feelings and sentiments of nine tenths of the people of this state.

We have planted the Standard of Liberty in Canada, for the attainment of the following objects:

Perpetual Peace, founded on a government of equal rights to all, secured by a written constitution, sanctioned by yourselves in a convention to be called as early as circumstances will permit.

Civil and Religious Liberty, in its fullest extent, that in all laws made, or to be made, every person be bound alike—neither shall any tenure, estate, charter, birth, or place, confer any exemption from the ordinary course of legal proceedings and responsibilities whereunto others are subjected.

The abolition of hereditary honours, of the laws of entail and primogeniture, and of hosts of pensioners who devour our substance.

A Legislature composed of a Senate and Assembly chosen by the people.

An Executive to be composed of a Governor and other officers elected by the public voice.

A Judiciary to be chosen by the Governor and Senate, and composed of the most learned, honourable, and trustworthy of our citizens. The laws to be rendered cheap and expeditious.

A free trial by Jury—Sheriffs chosen by you, and not to hold office, as now, at the pleasure of our tyrants. The freedom of the Press. Alas for it, now! The free presses in the Canadas are trampled down by the hand of arditrary power.

The vote by ballot—free and peaceful township elections.

The people to elect their court of request commissioners and justices of the peace—and also their militia officers, in all cases whatsoever.

Freedom of Trade—every man to be allowed to buy at the cheapest market, and sell at the dearest.

No man to be compelled to give military service, unless it be his choice.

Ample funds to be reserved from the vast natural resources of our country to secure the blessings of Education to every citizen.

A frugal and economical government, in order that the people may be prosperous and free from difficulty.

An end forever to the wearisome prayers, supplications and mockeries attendant upon our connexion with the Lordlings of the Colonial Office, Downing St. London.

The opening of the St. Lawrence to the trade of the world, so that the largest ships might pass up to Lake Superior, and the distribution of the wild lands of the country to the industry, capital, skill, and enterprise of worthy men of all nations.

For the attainment of these important objects, the patriots now in arms under the standard of Liberty, on NAVY ISLAND, U. C. have established a Provisional Government of which the members are as follows, (with two other distingnished gentlemen, whose names there are powful reasons for withholding from public view,) viz:

WILLIAM L. MACKENZIE, Chairman, Pro Tem.

NELSON GORHAM,	ADAM GRAHAM,
SAMUEL LOUNT,	JOHN HAWK,
SILAS FLETCHER,	JACOB RYMALL,
JESSE LLOYD,	WILLIAM H. DOYLE,
THOMAS DARLING,	A. G. W. G. VAN EGMOND.

CHARLES DUNCOMBE.

We have procured the important aid of Gen. Van Rensselaer of Albany, of Colonel Sutherland, Colonel Van Egmond, and other military men of experience; and the citizens of Buffalo, to their eternal honour be it ever remembered, have proved to us the enduring principles of the revolution of 1776, by supplying us with provisions, money, arms ammunition, artillery and volunteers; and vast numbers are floating to the standard under which, heaven willing, emancipation will be speedily won for a new and gallant nation, hitherto held in Egyptian thraldom by the aristocracy of England.

Brave Canadians! Hasten to join that standard, and to make common cause with your fellow citizens now in arms in the Home, London and Western Districts. The opportunity of the absence of the hired red coats of Europe is favourable to our emancipation. And short sighted is that man who does not now see that although his apathy may protract the contest, it must end in INDEPENDENCE, freedom from European thraldom for ever!

Until Independence is won, trade and industry will be dormant, houses and lands will be unsaleable, merchants will be embarrassed, and farmers and mechanicks harrassed and troubled; that point once gained, the prospect is fair and cheering, a long day of prosperity may be ours.

The reverses in the Home District were owing, 1st, to accident, which revealed our design to our tyrants, and prevented a surprise, and 2dly, to the want of artillery. 3500 men came and went, but we had not arms for one in twelve of them, nor could we procure them in the country.

Three hundred acres of the best of the publick lands will be freely bestowed upon any volunteer, who shall assist personally in bringing to a conclusion the glorious struggle in which our youthful country is now engaged against the enemies of freedom all the world over.

Ten millions of these lands, fair and fertile, will, I trust, be speedily at our disposal, with the other vast resources of a country more extensive and rich in natural treasurce than the United Kingdom or Old France.

Citizens! Soldiers of Liberty! Friends of Equal Rights, let no man suffer in his property, person or estate—let us pass through Canada, not to retaliate on others for our estates ravaged, our friends in dungeons, our homes burnt, our wheat and barns burnt, and our horses and cattle carried off; but let us show the praiseworthy example of protecting the houses, the homes, and the families of those who are in arms against their country and against the liberties of this continent. We will disclaim and severely punish all aggressions upon private property, and consider those as our enemies who may burn or destroy the smallest hut in Canada, unless necessity compel any one to do so in any cause for self defence.

Whereas, at a time when the King and Parliament of Great Britain had solemnly agreed to redress the grievances of the people, Sir Francis Bond Head was sent out to this country with promises of conciliation and justice—and whereas, the said Head hath violated his oath of office as a governor, trampled upon every vestige of our rights and privileges, bribed and corrupted the local legislature, interfered with the freedom of elections, intimidated the freeholders, declared our country not entitled to the blessings of British freedom, prostrated openly the right of trial by jury, placed in office the most obsequious, treacherous and unworthy, of our population—and sought to rule Upper Canada by the mere force of his arbitrary power, imprisoned Dr. Morrison, Mr. Parker, and many others of our most respected citizens, banishing in the most cruel manuer the highly respected speaker of our late House of Assembly, the Honorable Mr. Bidwell, and causing the expatriation of that universally beloved and well tried eminent patriot, Dr. John Rolph, because they had made common cause with our injured people, and setting a vast price on the heads of several, as if they were guilty persons—for which crimes and misdemeanors he is deserving of being put upon his trial before the country—I do therefore hereby offer a reward of FIVE HUNDRED POUNDS for his apprehension, so that he may be dealt with as may appertain to justice.

In Lower Canada, divine providence has blessed the arms of the Sons of Liberty—a whole people are there manfully struggling for that freedom without which property is but a phantom, and life scarce worth having a gift of. General Girard is at the head of 15,000 determined democrats.

The friends of freedom in Upper Canada, have continued to act in strong and regular concert with Mr. Papineau and the Lower Canada Patriots—and it is a pleasing reflection that between us and the ocean a population of 600,000 souls are now in arms, resolved to be free!

The tidings that worthy patriots are in arms is spreading through the Union, and the men who were oppressed in England, Ireland, Scotland and the continent are flocking to our standard.

We must be successful!

I had the honor to address nearly 3,000 of the citizens of Buffalo, two days ago, in the Theatre. The friendship and sympathy they expressed is honorable to the great and flourishing republic.

I am personally authorised to make known to you that from the moment that Sir Francis Head declined to state in writing the objects he had in view, in sending a flag of truce to our camp in Toronto, the message once declined, our esteemed fellow citizen Dr. John Rolph openly announced his concurrence in our measures, and now decidedly approves of the stand we are taking in behalf of our beloved country, which will never more be his until it be free and independent.

Canadians! my confidence in you is as strong and powerful, in this our day of trial and difficulty, as when, many years ago, in the zeal and ardour of youth, I appeared among you the humble advocate of your rights and liberties. I need not remind you of the sufferings and persecutions I have endured for your sakes—the losses I have sustained—the risks I have run. Had I ten lives I would cheerfully give them up to procure freedom to the country of my children, of my early and disinterested choice. Let us act together; and warmed by the hope of success in a patriotic course, be able to repeat in the language so often happily quoted by Ireland's champions,

The nations are fallen and thou still art young,
Thy sun is but rising when others have set;
And tho' Slavery's cloud o'er thy morning hath hung,
The full tide of Freedom shall beam round thee yet.

Militia-men of 1812! Will ye again rally round the standard of our tyrants! I can scarce believe it possible. Upper Canada Loyalists, what has been the recompense of your long tried and devoted attachment to England's Aristocracy? Obloquy, and contempt.

Verily we have learnt in the school of experience, and are prepared to profit by the lessons of the past. Compare the great and flourishing nation of the United States with our divided and distracted land, and think what we also might have been, as brave, independent lords of the soil. Leave then, Sir Francis Head's defence to the miserable serfs dependent on his bounty, and to the last hour of your lives the proud remembrance will be yours—"we also were among the deliverers of our country."

Navy Island, December, 13, 1837.

After the failure of his rebellion, Mackenzie fled to the United States and set up a provisional government on Navy Island in the Niagara River.

William Lyon Macken-zie, editor, politican, and leader of the 1837 rebellion in Upper Canada.

not come quickly enough or by peaceful means, staged a rebellion. He and Samuel Lount led the rebel forces — mostly farmers — down Yonge Street north of Toronto to the city. Their aim was to overthrow the government, but they were easily defeated.

Mackenzie fled and escaped to the United States. Other rebels did not escape; some were imprisoned, and some, like Samuel Lount, were hanged. Mackenzie was to return to Canada later under an official agreement that he would not be punished.

It was obvious to the British government that something was wrong. Lord Durham, an important aristocrat who strongly supported reform in Britain, was sent to Canada as Governor-in-Chief and High Commissioner to investigate the unrest. His *Report* condemned the Family Compact and recommended a better land granting system as well as the re-uniting of Upper and Lower Canada. It also called for "responsible government." Responsible government meant that the colonial Executive Council should answer to the Assembly: if the Executive lost the support of the majority of the Assembly, it would have to resign. The governor would have to take the advice of the responsible Executive. In this way the Assembly's voice would be the strongest in the government. Britain granted this important reform in 1848. It came because of changing attitudes in Britain along with the demands for it from Canadian political leaders.

Land Ownership in Upper Canada

You will remember that land ownership was very important to the new settlers of Upper Canada. The Constitutional Act had given them the system they wanted, but the way land was divided and sold or given out to settlers was to present many problems.

It was decided that land should be divided into townships. But portions of each township were to be set aside: one seventh for the clergy, known as *Clergy Reserves*, and one seventh for the Crown, known as *Crown Reserves*. This meant that over a quarter of the land in a township could not be settled.

The Clergy Reserves were intended for the support of the Protestant Clergy. In practice, this meant the Church of England. However, the majority of people in early Upper Canada belonged to churches other than the Church of England. It is understandable that they did not like Clergy Reserves.

Crown Reserves were to be a source of money for the provincial government. The Crown intended to hold its land until property values increased with an increase in settlers, and then sell or lease the reserves.

The reserve properties were scattered throughout a township. This got in the way of settlement and made it difficult to accomplish tasks that required co-operation. In almost one third of a township's lots, no one was responsible for such necessary activities as the building and clearing of roads, land drainage, or development.

In 1801, the government began offering Crown Reserves for lease. But people wanted to own their land, not rent it. And as long as there was plenty of land available to buy, which for many years there was, they had a choice.

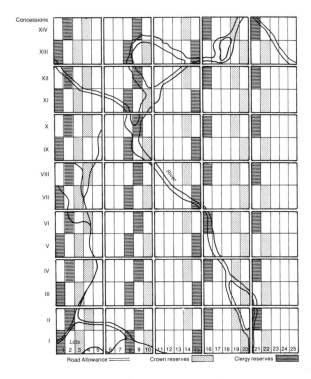

Crown and Clergy Reserves were scattered through a township in a chequer-board pattern. It is easy to see how they interfered with such co-operative undertakings as road building.

After the War of 1812 between Britain and the United States, large numbers of immigrants from overseas began arriving in Upper Canada and more leases were taken. But people complained that the reserves were blocking settlement. As early as 1817, members of the Assembly suggested that the reserves be sold. In 1825, the bulk of Upper Canada Crown reserves was sold to the Canada Company. In 1827, Clergy Reserves were permitted to be sold. Those people who had opposed Clergy Reserves all along wanted the money from their sale to go to education. This, and other issues related to land reserves, aroused many bitter feelings.

There was still another problem regarding land that proved even harder to solve than that of the reserves: it was difficult for the government to force private landowners to develop their land.

In the 1790s, many large areas of land became privately owned through land grants. Loyalist soldiers, who had supported the British government, were eligible for grants of 200 acres of land. Also, entire townships were granted to individuals who promised to bring in new settlers. By 1793, no less than twenty-five townships had been given away in this manner.

By 1796, many of these townships had been reclaimed by the government because the individuals had not fulfilled their promises about settlement. But there were still many large areas of land that had been given away which could not be reclaimed. And still more land was granted to government officials and prominent individuals.

Another way to acquire land was by buying *location tickets*. The "ticket" was a government certificate that allowed a settler to live on a piece of land in return for clearing and farming it. Once the settler had fulfilled these *settlement duties*, he could pay a fee and receive legal title to the land. This could take many years, however. Benjamin Wilson, believed to be the first settler in Ontario County, obtained his location ticket in 1796, but did not receive his patent, or title to the land, until 1819.

Certain people called speculators obtained land not for the purpose of farming, but in order to make a profit. They simply held on to the land until the value went up, and then sold it.

After 1812, the government tried to force owners to cultivate their property. In order to keep people from purchasing location tickets for the purpose of holding the land until a large profit could be made, Lieutenant Governor Maitland began to raise the fees charged for land grants. He also enforced settlement duties as another means of discouraging speculators. Maitland imposed taxes on wild lands, that is land not cleared, to force speculators to sell to people who would develop the land. But there were too few buyers for the vast areas for this to work.

Despite these and other changes in land regulations, people still acquired large holdings. In 1824, about eight million acres of privately owned land was undeveloped. In 1841, the amount had increased to over thirteen million. The problem continued after the Union Act of 1841 because the regulations of the new united government were weak. It was late in the 1840s before effective reforms began to be made.

The People of Upper Canada

The population of Upper Canada was made up mostly of people coming from Europe and the United States. In 1791, there were, however, some French-speaking settlers living on the Canadian side of the Detroit River. A few had also moved up the Thames River. These people followed the old system of narrow farms which stretched back from a river's shore. They were involved with fur trading as well as with farming.

There were also blacks living in Upper Canada at that time, but their numbers are not known. Nor is it known how many were free and how many were slaves. Although slavery existed, it was regarded as an evil institution. In 1793, Lieutenant Governor Simcoe had a law passed that would gradually abolish, or do away with, slavery. The black population increased as slaves escaped from bondage in the United States to freedom in Upper Canada.

Indian Settlements

Several thousand Chippewa and Mississauga Indians lived in Upper Canada before 1791. But the new settlers wanted land, and the British government began making treaties with the Indians to obtain their land for the settlers. By 1838, the government had gained title to most of what is now southern Ontario.

Some of the land that the British obtained was given to other Indians. There were the Iroquois, or Six Nation Indians, who came to Upper Canada in 1784 as Loyalists. A group under

After the American Revolution, Chief Joseph Brant led the loyalist Mohawk tribe to the area of the Grand River where he was given a large grant of land.

Captain John Deseronto received land on the Bay of Quinte. Another group, under Chief Joseph Brant, received a grant six miles wide along the Grand River. This land was a reward for supporting the British and a compensation for land lost in their former home.

Brant realized that the Six Nation Indians could not farm all the land they had received, about 570,000 acres. He decided to sell some of it so the Indians could benefit financially. At first the government opposed Brant's proposal for fear that the Indians would be tricked into selling the land for a price below its real worth. But in 1798, the government agreed to accept the sales Brant made. Over half the grant, approximately 350,000 acres, passed out of Indian control. As more settlers came to Upper Canada, they wanted to purchase other Iroquois land. Sometimes squatters settled the land without first buying it. Problems with Indian land continued until 1841 when the British Crown took over the lands the Indians were farming plus a reserve of 20,000 acres. Any extra land in the original grant would be sold by the government, and the profit would be put into an account for the benefit of the Indians.

There were problems with other Indian lands. The Moravians, a group of Indians who had been converted to Christianity, came to Upper Canada in 1792. They settled along the Thames River and established Fairfield, also known as Moraviantown. By government orders of 1793 and 1798, the Indians were

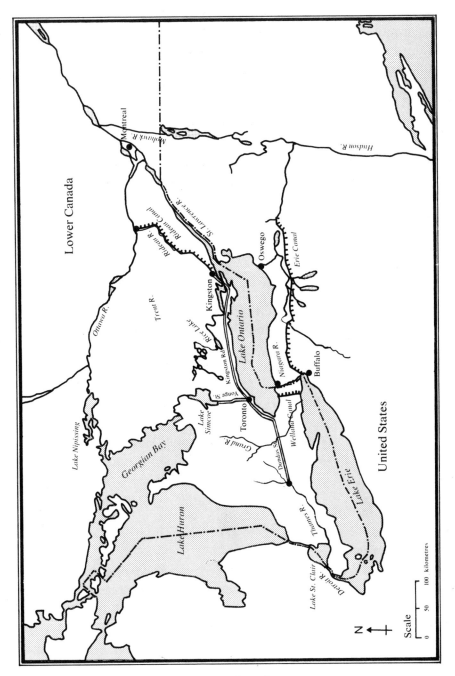

The main roads and waterways of Upper Canada.

granted a reserve of about 50,000 acres. The Moravian Indians lived mainly by farming, but they also traded maple sugar, corn, and other products with white settlers. During the War of 1812, American forces destroyed their village. The Indians returned to the area in August, 1815, and established New Fairfield on the opposite side of the river from the old village.

The new village grew slowly, and most of the reserve was left uncultivated. White settlers in the area complained. Several times the Indians refused government requests to sell the reserve. Finally, in 1837, they agreed to sell half of it. In the same year, most of the Indians left New Fairfield for the United States. The remainder stayed on under the leadership of Moravian missionaries. But the population increased very slowly and had only reached just over 250 in the 1840s. In 1857, the Indians surrendered the rest of the reserve, about 22,000 acres, leaving each remaining family with a farm of about 40 acres.

The Mohawks, one of the Six Nations on the Grand River, were Christian converts, and the governor promised to provide them with a church and school. The church was built in 1785, the first Protestant church in Upper Canada. Known as Her Majesty's Chapel of the Mohawks, it is still standing near Brantford. No school was provided until almost 1820. But neither church nor school saved the Six Nations from the problems that harmed all Indians in Upper Canada.

The Indian way of life was gradually disappearing. It was undermined by European culture and goods. Unable and unwilling to adapt to a European style society, the Indian family and social organization began to break down. European diseases were also a strong threat to Indians, who did not have immunity to these foreign illnesses.

Problems of health, adaptation, and land possession were just beginning for the Indians when Upper Canada was created in 1791. The Indians would never become a part of the white settlers' development of the province.

Loyalists and "Late Loyalists"
United Empire Loyalists were the largest group of settlers before

The church shown in this sketch of the Mohawk Village was the first Protestant church in Upper Canada. Known today as Her Majesty's Chapel of the Mohawks, it can still be seen near Brantford.

1791. A few settled on the west side of the Niagara River as early as 1776, but the majority came in 1783 and 1784. They left the United States because they did not support the War of Independence against Britain. Many had their land and homes taken away by American patriots. They came to Canada with few possessions. The government gave these new settlers land, tools, and seed to start farming, and later, money as compensation for what they had lost in the United States.

About 6,000 Loyalists settled along the St. Lawrence River west of Montreal, from Kingston to the Bay of Quinte, and at the western end of Lake Ontario. Loyalists were Americans of English, Scottish, German, French, and Native origin. They came primarily from New York, Pennsylvania, and New Jersey. Because many had experience with pioneer life, they soon created thriving farms and communities.

In many ways, the history of Upper Canada began with the

Most Loyalists arrived with few possessions. As they found themselves surrounded by the most absolute wilderness, the task of clearing the land and establishing a home must have seemed enormous.

Loyalists. They brought more than different ways of farming, different forms of government, and large numbers. They brought new attitudes that distinguished them from other settlers of Canada. One important attitude was their desire to remain under British rule. But while they often stressed loyalty to Britain and the Crown, they wanted to run their local affairs without interference from Britain. Their attitudes toward the United States were complex too. On the one hand, they loved the land where many of them had been born, had farmed, and still had relatives. Yet they disliked the American form of government. All of these attitudes existed in Upper Canada, and indeed, many have lasted up to the present.

The Loyalists opened the way for thousands of immigrants from the United States. Their relatives, friends, and neighbors heard about the good farmlands, low taxes, and absence of danger from Indian wars. They also learned how easy it was to get land. When Lieutenant Governor Simcoe stated the requirements in a proclamation of February, 1792, he made sure that the terms were publicized in New England, New York, and Pennsylvania. The land was to be surveyed into townships, as it was in the United States. A lot of 200 acres would be granted in return for an oath of allegiance to the King, the payment of small fees to cover the costs of the grant, and a promise to clear and cultivate the land. Here is an example of what the settlers were to do:

> They must within the term of two years clear fit for cultivation and fence, ten acres of the lot obtained; build a house 16 by 20 feet of logs or frame, with a shingle roof; also cut down all timber in front of and the whole width of the lot . . . 33 feet of which must be cleared smooth and left for half the public road.

An additional 1,000 acres could be granted at the government's discretion. This land would be owned outright, in freehold tenure, in accordance with the British system.

Most of the American settlers who came to Canada after the Loyalists came for land, although a few came because they preferred to live in a British colony. Sometimes, the American immigrants of the late 1780s and early 1790s are called "late Loyalists." The War of 1812 stopped the immigration of Americans. Even after the War, the British and provincial governments discouraged American immigration for fear that the settlers would not be loyal to the Crown. The argument over this policy lasted until 1827. Among the government's opponents were large landowners who wanted to sell lands to American settlers. Also, many reformers supported the cause of American immigrants. Nevertheless, the influx of Americans did decline after 1815 because of the government's policy. Also, American settlers were attracted to the new lands opening in Ohio and further west in the United States.

Successes and Failures

Whatever their motives and loyalties, the American immigrants proved to be excellent pioneers. They had the knowledge, skills,

Conestoga wagons were designed primarily to move freight, but they also proved to be an ideal means of transportation for settlers. Their name comes from the area in Pennsylvania where they originated.

and willingness to clear the forest and could exist with all the hardships of settling in the wilderness.

Quakers from New England moved into the Niagara Peninsula, beginning in the 1780s, and into York County in the 1790s. Mennonites from Pennsylvania, who were mainly German-speaking, came to the same areas about the same time and, after 1801, they settled in Waterloo County. Accompanying them were Dunkards, another religious group of German-speaking people from Pennsylvania. Settlers of Scottish origin came from New York and Pennsylvania. Baptists, Methodists, and, beginning in 1786, Roman Catholics from Scotland came too.

Those who came in groups had many advantages over individual settlers. They helped each other clear land, build houses, and harvest crops. They looked after each other when someone became sick or was hurt. They supplied their own churches and schools. A group could establish a new community more quickly than individual settlers who were strangers to one another.

Many American pioneers approached the problem of settling in Upper Canada in a systematic way. They did not simply arrive and take the first land offered them. Instead, experienced farmers would come, carefully choose a location, build a log cabin, and plant wheat. These men might spend one or two years in Upper Canada, or they might return home and every year visit Upper Canada to sow and harvest crops. When they had found suitable land, the rest of their group would move, usually bringing enough money with them to get their farms started.

Thomas Choate came from New Hampshire to Wentworth County in 1796. During the next two years, he returned to New Hampshire several times, coming back to Upper Canada to plant crops in the spring and harvest them in the fall. In 1798 he migrated with three brothers and two cousins to settle permanently. Timothy Rogers, a Quaker from Vermont, visited Upper Canada in 1800 and arranged for a land grant. The next year, he brought in forty families who settled where Newmarket is now. In 1800, Joseph Sherk and Samuel Betzner came on behalf of Pennsylvania Mennonites. They liked an area on the upper part of the Grand River, originally part of the Six Nations grant, and within a year or two their group had bought 60,000 acres in what became Waterloo County. An influx of settlers from Pennsylvania to Waterloo began in 1801 and continued for many years. They came in Conestoga wagons, which were so well built they could sometimes be floated across small rivers.

American immigrants continued what the Loyalists had begun — the peopling of Upper Canada. As more people came, they introduced greater variety into the religious life of the province. Settlements north of York, now Toronto, and in Waterloo County were important because they were the first movements of people inland, away from the lakes. This began the clearing of the backwoods of Upper Canada. As these capable pioneers opened new lands, more and more people were attracted.

Immigrants also came from the British Isles, especially from Scotland. Many were driven out of their homelands by poverty and hunger. Others who left were not so desperate but hoped nonetheless to improve their condition by emigrating to Canada. Some were encouraged by letters from relatives and friends who had already moved to Canada. Many people heard about the advantages of emigrating to British North America from agents who travelled around the British Isles speaking and distributing pamphlets and books. These agents talked about the good land, the opportunities, and the freedom to be found in Canada. People often were not told about the difficulties, the hard work, and long hours necessary to establish a farm. Or, perhaps, they did not believe such warnings.

Some attempts at settlement achieved little success or even failed. William Berczy had brought German settlers to New York state. When he heard about Simcoe's offer of lands in Upper Canada, he formed the German Company to carry out settlement. The government of Upper Canada granted him 64,000 acres on the Rouge River east of York. The first settlers arrived in the winter of 1794–95, a very difficult time to begin pioneering. Although he built sawmills and gristmills, his efforts did not succeed. The settlement hardly grew at all. In 1797, the government took back the undeveloped land. The few German settlers who remained continued their hard struggle. They were the founders of Markham.

Another unsuccessful settlement attempt was led by a French nobleman who had fled from the French Revolution. The Comte de Puisaye persuaded the British government to send a group of noblemen, called *émigrés*, to Upper Canada and support them for three years. The provincial government gave them a large grant, including 5,000 acres for de Puisaye, north of York. To this area, called Windham Settlement, came about 40 émigrés. They were completely unfit to undertake pioneering work and they soon lost heart. By 1802, only thirteen remained, and the next year the government took back the lands that had not been developed.

At the turn of the century, the majority of immigrants were coming from the United States. There were men who did not like this situation. They asked for large land grants so that they could attract British settlers. One of them was Lord Selkirk, a Scottish nobleman, who was granted 1,200 acres, plus 150 for each family he settled. Each colonist was to receive 50 acres at Baldoon, near Lake St. Clair. The first settlers came in 1804, but there were problems from the very beginning. The land was marshy and flooded easily. The first year the crops were flooded; the next year they were hit by drought. Many people fell ill from malaria and several died. It is not surprising the settlers became discouraged and did not work hard. Also, they did not have Selkirk

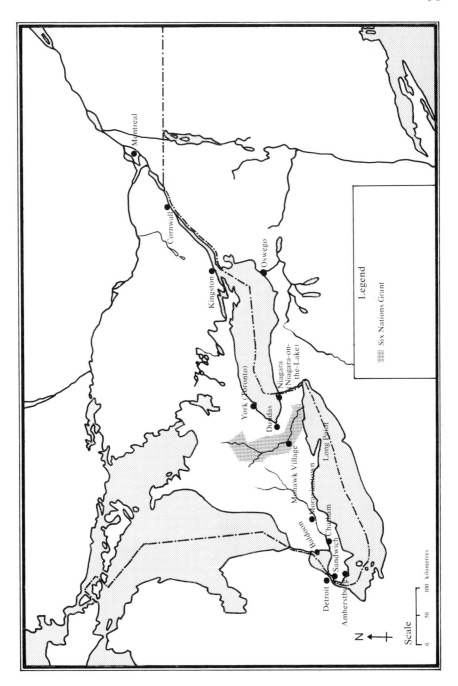

Upper Canada was very sparsely populated in 1805.

there to encourage them. He had remained in Scotland and left the management of the settlement to an incompetent agent. Few of the settlers stayed, and Selkirk withdrew his support before 1812.

New Settlers Come from Overseas

By 1812, Upper Canada's population was between 75,000 and 80,000. One reliable source states that three out of every five people were either natives of the United States or their children. In other words, without American immigration, Upper Canada would have been much more of a wilderness than it was. On the eve of the War of 1812, Upper Canada's population was mixed, but it was primarily English-speaking, Protestant in religion, and North American in character. After the War, with changes in immigration, the character became more European.

The first accurate census of Upper Canada, taken in 1851, established the population at 952,000. Before that date there are only guesses about the number of people. These suggest, however, that the population in 1821 was about 100,000; in 1824 about 150,000; and in 1838 about 400,000. More important than actual figures, however, was the trend: population was increasing, and the numbers took a big jump in the 1830s.

Population grew mainly because of immigration. Between 1815 and 1841 about 600,000 emigrants left Britain for British North America. How many remained permanently in Upper Canada is unknown. The problem is that many people came to Canada not to settle but to move on to the United States. No accurate count was made of arrivals in and departures from Upper Canada.

In Europe there had been a long war during which thousands of men were in the army. In 1815, after the fighting ended, many soldiers could not find enough work. At the same time, machines and factories were replacing the old ways of producing cloth. Weavers and spinners had less and less to do. Even when they had work, wages were too low to support their families. Farmers with only a small amount of land could no longer make a living because prices dropped. Unemployed people, called paupers, begged or depended on government assistance to live. This led British government officials and others to think the country was over-populated. Officials feared political disturbances, and perhaps even revolution.

To relieve poverty, reduce over-population, and eliminate causes for political discontent, the British government helped groups of people to emigrate. It had another important reason for sending some of these to Canada. The War of 1812 with the United States had stopped American immigration. But Canada needed people to develop and strengthen the country. More British emigration to Canada would help the colony, as well as Britain and the British Empire. The British government paid the costs of the emigrants' journey and, in some cases, the expenses of getting settled.

In 1815 and 1816, about 1,400 former soldiers and Scottish laborers and farmers were sent to Upper Canada and settled in Lanark County, west of the Rideau River. Besides paying the cost of the voyage, the government gave 100 acres to each father of a family and promised the same to each male child when he reached age twenty-one. Free rations were also provided for a short period, along with axes and other farm tools at reduced prices. The government promised to pay the salaries of a clergyman and school teacher. To discourage immigrants from simply moving on to the United States, the government required a deposit which would be returned to settlers after two years if they were still living on their land.

The areas of settlement had much rocky and swampy land which discouraged some immigrants, particularly the soldiers, who drifted away. But the Scots around Perth persisted. In 1820 and 1821 about 2,500 Scots, mainly weavers, established the New Lanark settlement. These immigrants had no pioneering experience, and they had to turn heavily forested, rocky soil into farms. It took years of hard struggle before they began to prosper, but by the 1830s this Rideau settlement had about 18,000 people and was a success.

In 1823, Peter Robinson was asked by the British government to supervise the emigration of poor Irish farmers and laborers. He brought 571 settlers from County Cork and settled them between Perth and the Ottawa River in Lanark County. Two years later, he brought 2,000 more people from the same area of Ireland and settled them north of Rice Lake. These people founded Peterborough, named after Robinson. The government provided 100 acres to each family and to each son aged twenty-one; built a log house on each lot; provided rations of pork and flour for eighteen months; gave each family a cow, tools, seed, and even a cooking pot. A priest arrived in 1826. The settlers soon established prosperous farms. Their settlement succeeded because of hard work, Robinson's planning and leadership, and government help during the first, most difficult years.

The government had other ways of encouraging emigration at little or no expense to itself. For example, it settled soldiers in Upper Canada. Sometimes it disbanded regiments in Canada, which saved the cost of transporting the men back to Britain and paying them pensions there. This was done in 1818 with the 99th Regiment. The men were sent up the Ottawa River to settle in Carleton County. They were given land, a small amount of money, rations for a year, and tools. They established Richmond which, by 1820, had become a flourishing village. The government also sent pensioners to Canada. These were soldiers who had left the army and were receiving payments from the government. They could exchange their pensions for a sum of money, free passage to Canada, and a land grant. Between 1830 and 1839, 1,000 to 1,500 pensioners came to Upper Canada. They settled in different parts of the province, with the largest numbers in Dummer Township, Peterborough County and Medonte Township, Simcoe County.

This method of settlement was not successful. No more than half the pensioners stayed on their lands and established farms. Some were too old or ill to do the hard work of pioneering. Many did not know how. As one pensioner said: "Some wouldn't sit down on their land at all, they lost all heart to see everywhere trees, and trees, and nothing beside. And then they didn't know nothing of farming ... how should they, being

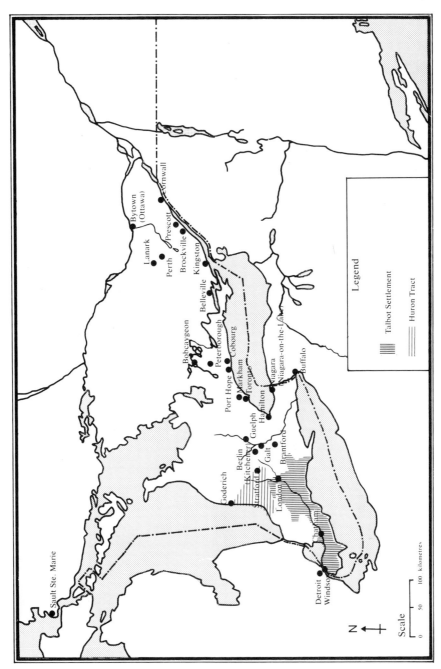

By 1841, there were many towns and villages in Upper Canada and the population had greatly increased.

Thomas Talbot began his career as colonizer with a grant of 5,000 acres. Thirty years later he controlled 65,000 acres and had settled thousands of people.

soldiers by trade?'' Many who left their land did not have a trade and ended up in Toronto, living in terrible poverty, ''begging in the streets with their children, and inhabiting hovels in the most unhealthy parts of town.''

Leaders of Settlement

The government also encouraged immigration by granting or selling land to men who promised to promote immigration and settlement. William Dickson was one such individual who played an important role in bringing settlers to Upper Canada. Dickson made money as a merchant and bought land northwest of Hamilton. To attract immigrants from his native Scotland, he advertised there and sent an agent to talk to people. As settlers arrived, he helped them to get started. He hired Absalom Shade, from Pennsylvania, to supervise the settlement. Shade energetically built mills, roads, and schools, and he established Shade's Mills, which Dickson renamed Galt.

The most famous individual promoter of colonization was Colonel Thomas Talbot. In 1803, Talbot received a land grant of 5,000 acres on the north shore of Lake Erie. Additional land was set aside in the area for a settlement that Talbot was to promote. The government agreed to allow him 200 acres of land for each settler he placed on 50 acres. He made little progress before 1812, by which time he had only placed about thirty families. His main success came after the War of 1812. By 1836, Talbot had 28 townships under his supervision, stretching 130 miles from Long Point to the Detroit River and north to the Huron Tract. He had settled about 40,000 people. He attracted immigrants from New York, Scotland, and the Red River in Rupert's Land, now Manitoba. He also saw to the building of nearly 300 miles of excellent (for the time) roads.

This was one of the keys to his success. He realized that his settlers would need good roads to link their backwoods farms with towns. The way to get them built was to require that pioneers fulfill their settlement duties. These duties were not enforced in other parts of Upper Canada and settlers suffered from the lack of good roads.

Talbot insisted that settlers clear half the road in front of their lots, clear ten acres of their farms, and build a house. Not only did they have to chop the trees to clear the road but they also had to keep their road open all year long. After five years, if the settler had fulfilled his duties and remained on his land, Talbot would give him a certificate which he could exchange for a legal title.

Talbot got into trouble with the government of Upper Canada which thought he was claiming more land than he should have been and that he acted as a dictator over his settlers. He upset provincial officials because several times he appealed to the British government for support against them. Talbot did pretty much as he pleased in his settlement. Applicants for land had to see Talbot personally at his house. When they came, he slid open a small window and discussed business through it. When he granted a piece of land, he wrote the name in pencil on a plan. If the settler neglected his duties or displeased him for some other reason, Talbot simply erased the name. Yet, despite his strange ways, Talbot was sympathetic and helpful to poor settlers and took no fees for granting land. As he got older and more eccentric, he could no longer manage the affairs of such a large settlement. In 1837, the government asked him to organize his records and give up his authority. Talbot agreed to end his role as a colonizer, but it was not until after his death in 1853 that the government obtained all his records.

For his colonization work, the government granted Talbot the townships of Dunwich and Aldborough, about 40,000 acres altogether. He did not clear the land or open much of it for settlement, which caused some of the nearby settlers to complain. Although he received a small pension, beginning in 1826, and a percentage of certain land sales, he was not a rich man. He had spent £20,000, settled thousands of farmers, and built the finest roads in Upper Canada at no expense to the government. Until 1833, he lived in a simple log cabin. By selling some cattle he was able to build a new log house nearby. It stood on a high cliff above Lake Erie and from his sitting room he could watch the lake. The room's walls were bare logs — no paint or wallpaper — and its only furniture was a long table, a desk, bookshelves, and two home-made wooden chairs. There is a legend that he had a mark on the wall and when the sun's rays reached it, he would start drinking liquor for the rest of the day. In 1837, a visitor said of Talbot: "He is alone — a lonely man ... "

Companies were also formed to promote settlement. The most important of these was the Canada Company. It was founded in 1825 and received over a million acres of Crown Reserves and the Huron Tract, a total of more than two million acres of land, in return for a large payment to the provincial government. The company quickly began ambitious programs of road building, school building, and public works to attract settlers.

The first secretary and superintendent of the Company, John Galt, and another official, William "Tiger" Dunlop, arrived in Upper Canada in 1827. Both were writers from Scotland. They were enthusiastic about the job that awaited them, and in April of that year began clearing land that would later become Guelph.

The Canada Company succeeded in attracting immigrants and successfully settling them, and it established the towns of

MAP OF THE TOWNSHIPS IN THE PROVINCE OF UPPER CANADA.

LANDS IN UPPER CANADA,

TO BE DISPOSED OF BY THE

CANADA COMPANY.

INCORPORATED BY ROYAL CHARTER AND ACT OF PARLIAMENT, IN 1826.

The Canada Company was founded in 1825. By the time its contract with the government ended in 1843, it had played a major role in colonizing the western part of Upper Canada.

Guelph, Stratford and Goderich. It gained critics as well as supporters, however. One opponent of The Company was William Lyon Mackenzie, who attacked it because it gave financial support to the Family Compact.

A Cross-Section of Society

Most of the settlers who came to Upper Canada in the 1820s and 1830s were poor and most were from the British Isles. Although fares across the Atlantic were low, some were too poor to pay their own way. They were helped by money sent from relatives, or by aid from their parish. Sometimes landlords paid the costs of sending their tenants overseas.

Wealthy people from Britain also came, however. Some came for the adventure, others to escape high taxes or because they feared their standard of living would decline. There were professional men, farmers, and officers who had left the army or navy and were living on reduced pay. In Canada, they could obtain large land grants and positions in government. A few brought enough money to hire laborers to clear their land and servants for their homes. They enjoyed good food and imported furniture. But most had to do some of the hard work of pioneering themselves. Not all succeeded. Some returned to Britain, others moved to towns, but enough remained in the backwoods to create small centres of genteel British society.

These people included three members of the Strickland family who settled in the Trent region of Peterborough County. Major Samuel Strickland arrived in 1825. After working for the Canada Company, he established a farm near Lakefield and a lumber business. His sisters, Catharine Traill and Susanna Moodie, came with their husbands in 1832. Mr. and Mrs. Traill took up land in Douro Township and the Moodies settled nearby. The Moodies did not like pioneering and soon moved to Belleville. There was also Mrs. Frances Stewart who settled with her husband, Thomas, in Douro Township. Mr. Stewart owned a large amount of land and became a member of the Legislative Council. There were many others, such as James Wallis who founded Fenelon Falls, land speculator John Langton and his sister, Thomas Need who established a sawmill which was the beginning of the settlement of Bobcaygeon, and Hamnet Pinhey, a merchant on the Ottawa River.

Often these people wrote books about their experiences. They described their own lives and feelings and the society around them. The fact that they wrote books indicates that they were educated and had some time free from daily work. People in Europe must have been interested in reading about life in North America because many books, pamphlets, and newspaper articles were written. Visitors to North America also wrote books about their travels and usually included a section of advice to possible emigrants. This flood of printed material encouraged emigration and may have influenced where in North America some people went.

A number of settlers also came from continental Europe. People who wanted to escape poverty, find freedom of religion, or just have a change, hoped they could find a new life in North America. For example, the religious group known as the Amish came from Germany to Waterloo County in 1824 to escape military service. The next year, a large migration of Lutherans and Catholics from southern Germany began for the same reason. Most went to the United States, but many came to Waterloo County and established farms and businesses. They contributed to the development of Ebytown, later known as Berlin, and now as Kitchener.

As you can see, Upper Canada was settled by many different kinds of people, with many different reasons for coming. It benefited from the influx of Americans and Europeans. Roads, bridges, harbors and canals had to be built. Schools, churches, libraries and hospitals were needed. Businesses of many kinds were started. To those born in Canada as well as to those who came from foreign lands, Canada was a land of opportunity.

Life on a Pioneer Farm

If you had taken a boat trip up the St. Lawrence River and along Lakes Ontario and Erie during the 1790s, you would have seen nearly all the settlements of Upper Canada. Most settlers were farmers, and because there were few good roads, they lived close to water routes.

Starting a Farm

Early pioneers had to clear vast amounts of forested land before they could begin farming. They cut down the trees and used what they needed for building. The rest they either burned or sold as lumber. The burned wood could be used to make charcoal, or the ashes, called potash, could be sold to make soap or gunpowder.

Pioneers did not have machinery to help them clear the land; it was a difficult process and often took years to complete. The roots of large trees had to be left to rot for several years before they could be removed from the ground. Stones could be put to good use in building fences, but this too took a great deal of time.

Money and equipment were scarce, so farmers had to make use of any materials that were available. If they were to succeed, they had to be skilled in many things, not only in farming. Even if a farmer did have some money, few tools were available in the sparsely settled areas of Upper Canada.

The main crops in the early days were corn and wheat. In some areas, such as the Niagara Peninsula, fruit growing was started. These crops were sold throughout Upper and Lower

Thomas W. Magrath (Erindale Toronto) to
Rev. Thomas Radcliff (Dublin) Jan., 1832.

The land has a miserable appearance when first cleared, the surface and stumps being as black as fire can render them, and these latter standing three feet high, to facilitate their being drawn out by two yoke of oxen when their roots decay, which does not take effect for seven or eight years, (according to the kind of timber) and is more tedious if the land be laid down for grass.

Our first agricultural proceedings are as rude and simple as can well be imagined. A triangular harrow, the teeth of which weigh 7 lbs. each, is dragged over the newly prepared ground; its irregular and jumping passage over the roots and loose vegetable earth scatters the ashes of the burned timber over the entire surface; the wheat is then sown, about one bushel to the acre, and another scrape of the harrow completes the process.

On some portion of his land thus cleared, the new settler plants potatoes, turnips, pumpkins and Indian corn, merely laying the seed upon the ground, and, with a hoe, scratching a sufficient portion of earth and ashes to cover it—a luxuriant crop generally succeeds; in this district from twenty to thirty bushels of wheat per acre . . .

After wheat, no other crop is taken (generally speaking) except hay, until after the removal of the [tree] roots, when the ploughs can work.

A pioneer writes about early farming.

Canada. Other farmers grew vegetables, or raised animals. Many people kept small vegetable gardens for their own food supply.

Wild fruits, nuts, berries, and plants were gathered and used because of their abundance. But as settlements grew, these wild crops were destroyed.

Even more than today, farmers were at the mercy of the weather. There was little they could do if there was too much rain, or an early frost. For example, from 1835 to 1838 poor weather caused such low crop yield that some backwoods farmers almost starved.

Insects and disease were also problems to these early farmers. There were no chemical sprays to kill insects nor were cures known for plant diseases. In 1790, when the wheat crops were attacked by Hessian flies, there was little that could be done. Farmers could only hope that they would harvest their crops before disaster struck. A few, if they could afford it, switched from an unsuccessful crop to a more promising one. But most were forced to continue with the crops they had begun growing.

People were concerned with the most basic needs: food, shelter, and clothing. Their farms had to produce enough crops if they were to meet these basic needs. After a crop had been grown for several years, the soil would lose its nutrients and the crops would become weak. Many pioneer farmers would abandon the land and seek new locations because their land was worn out and they could get better land.

Some farmers, even in these early days, followed more careful methods of farming. They would maintain the soil's fertility by rotating crops or by allowing a piece of land to lie fallow, or unused, for a few years. This allowed the soil to regain its nutrients.

In the same way, methods of raising farm animals were improved. At first animals were left to wander in the woods to find their own food, but gradually farmers began taking better care of their animals. First they fenced them in and then they began raising feed crops. In this way, the production of livestock increased significantly.

Slowly, farm tools were also improved. With labor-saving machinery, farmers could clear fields more quickly, plant more crops, and have more time to make other improvements to their farms. Those in more settled areas often had access to better tools. Ploughs and grain-cradles were available for harvesting and planting. As better ploughs, harrows, and reapers were introduced into Upper Canada from the United States and Britain, harvesting became easier. A single farmer could thresh between eight and sixteen bushels of grain a day using a simple tool called a flail, while a threshing machine could thresh fifty bushels an hour.

People who were not farmers were interested in the problems faced by farmers because they were very dependent upon them. Today food is obtained from all over the world. If one region of the world suffers from a drought, it is likely that food can be imported from elsewhere. The relationship between the farmer and the buyer is indirect. In pioneer times, townspeople often bought their food straight from the local farmers. If crops were good, prices fell. If crops were poor, prices rose and people went short of food.

In early pioneer days, a wooden flail was used to thresh grain. Later, this horse-powered threshing machine got the job done much faster.

Farmers found many ways to make use of horsepower to lighten their work. Here we see horses being used to run a machine for sawing logs.

The Problems Farmers Faced

Can you think of some problems a farmer in the 1830s or 1840s might have faced?

To begin with, they faced long hours of heavy manual labor. This was especially true for backwoods farmers who had few tools to make their work easier. Before he could begin planting, a farmer had to clear the land, build a cabin, and prepare the soil. It could take years and years to clear an entire farm of 200 acres.

Besides the farm work, families had to be cared for. Furniture was made by hand, as was clothing; all foods were made and stored or canned from basic ingredients. Children were often taught at home, in between their chores, and there were church and community activities to attend.

Given this amount of work, helpers were very important. Every member of a family contributed to the running of the house and farm. Families were often large so that there would be many people to help. But when children grew up and left home, there were few outside helpers to replace them. Often money was too scarce to hire those people who were available.

For the backwoods farmer, isolation was a major problem. Because there were few good roads, it was difficult to travel from the isolated farms to more settled centres. Travel was actually easiest in the winter, when sleighs could be used. During the rest of the year, the unpaved roads were so muddy that wagons would get stuck.

Walking was often the fastest and safest means of transportation. Pioneers expected to walk long distances, carrying their goods on their backs. This limited the amount of goods that could be transported in a single trip.

Farmers who lived beside lakes or rivers could use boats for transportation. But this too was often dangerous or inconvenient. In dry seasons rivers could become too shallow for boats, and in rainy seasons the current could be too fast for a trip to be made safely.

It is easy to see that establishing a home and life in early Upper Canada took a great deal of work, dedication, and co-operation.

Removing stumps was a major problem in clearing the land. This horse-operated apparatus made the task much easier.

Visiting a Pioneer Home

Try to imagine a home in early Upper Canada. What would it look like? What kind of furniture would it have? How would it be heated in the winter? What would the people eat and wear? What might the family be doing on an average day?

Most likely, the house would be built of wood. The first houses were built of round logs because these required the least preparation. If a settler had more time and money, the house might be built of squared logs. Simple frame houses with boards on the outside followed next. But the preparation of boards was difficult and took a long time when done by hand. Sawmills made this work easier. There were a few stone and brick houses, but most of them were in villages.

Throughout the early 1800s, logs remained the main building material for homes because they were cheap and available. But log houses were not very comfortable. There were always gaps between round logs. These spaces had to be filled — or chinked — with mud or lime plaster which had to be replaced every year. Also, as the wood dried, it shrank, which made the gaps even wider. Houses often settled, or shifted, and usually not evenly. As a result, floors and walls tilted and doors and windows stuck. Square logs fitted more closely, but they still had to be chinked. They presented the same problems as they dried and settled.

Some houses had windows with glass. The poor, who could not afford glass, either had few windows or, instead of glass, they used oiled paper or rags. Glass was expensive because it was imported. It became cheaper after 1825 when it began to be manufactured in Upper Canada.

Inside the House

You probably entered a house from a verandah, or porch, which settlers built to protect their houses from the sun in summer and cold winds in winter. An early log cabin might have only one room. In this, the family cooked, ate, slept, entertained, and did household chores. Sometimes, two rooms were created by hanging a blanket or curtain or by putting up a rough board partition. This provided some privacy for sleeping.

All cooking was done in the huge fireplace of a settler's first house. Even bread was baked there, in a lidded iron pot which was covered with coals and ashes.

Frame, brick, or stone houses had several rooms. Large houses were usually not built of logs because the construction was not secure enough to support the size. A large house would have a cellar for the storage of fruit and vegetables during the winter. On the ground floor, you would probably see the dining room on one side of a main hall and a sitting room, called a drawing room or parlor, on the other. Upstairs you would find either two or four bedrooms. If the hall was wide, it might be used as a sitting room or for some activity like sewing, spinning, or weaving. The bathroom was an outside privy.

The kitchen was sometimes located behind the dining room, but more likely it was right at the back of the house, in a separate wing, or even in the cellar. The reason for putting the kitchen away from the main part of the house was the heat that its big fireplace produced. Kitchen fireplaces had to be huge, four feet or more wide. This heat was welcome in the winter, but in the summer it could make the house unbearable.

In a one-room cabin, the fireplace was used for heating and cooking. Early fireplaces were very crude. The fire would be on the ground or on a bed of stones. There might be a hole in the roof to let the smoke out or a simple chimney made of clay and long, thin strips of wood called laths. These chimneys caught fire easily.

It was important to keep the fire in the fireplace burning. There were no matches in those days, and someone would have to go to a neighbor's to get a live ember. This could be a problem if the nearest neighbor was miles away! Even in the heat of summer, the fire had to be kept going for cooking.

Larger houses had separate fireplaces in the main rooms: dining room, sitting room, and front, upstairs bedrooms. The other rooms were unheated. In winter, even rooms with fireplaces were cold. Settlers wrote about water freezing in a glass on the dinner table, water freezing overnight in bedrooms, and windows covered inside with heavy frost. This happened in well built houses, not only in log cabins.

At first, stoves were scarce and expensive. But gradually they began replacing fireplaces for cooking. Stove pipes were run through walls and across rooms to provide a little extra warmth. By the 1820s, stoves were being manufactured in Upper Canada, and by the 1840s they had replaced fireplaces as a means of heating homes.

The floors in early houses were usually covered with strips of bark or smoothed half-logs. But occasionally, in very poor houses, the floor was only dirt. Floors were uneven and poorly constructed. Settlers soon replaced such crude floors with thick boards pegged to beams below by wooden dowels. Unpainted floors were cleaned by scrubbing with wet sand, which made the wood shine. Or, if there was a little more money, the floor could be covered with paint or rugs. Paint was expensive and in short supply, and rugs took a long time to make.

Furniture varied as much as houses. The wealthy could afford fine imported furniture, while the middle class and poor

When time permitted, a settler might build an outdoor bake oven. The loaves of bread were put in and removed with a long-handled wooden shovel called a peel.

usually made their own. Tables, benches, and beds were most often made from pine wood. Benches might also serve as beds, and they usually had a hinged lid so things could be stored inside. Closets or wardrobes were not common. Clothes and other articles were hung on pegs on the wall. Beds were simply constructed, and mattresses might be made of elm bark, pine boughs, or a large bag, called a tick, filled with straw. Later, ticks were filled with duck or goose feathers, which made a more comfortable mattress.

As people had more money to spend on extras, better furniture was bought from local craftsmen. There were many fine furniture makers who copied styles from Britain and elsewhere. Chairs and sofas stuffed with wool replaced benches, tables of rough boards and crude beds gave way to drop-leaf tables of walnut or cherry and four-poster beds. Chests and cupboards took the place of pegs.

Pine furniture was often painted bright colors, red being a favorite. Houses could be dreary and cold, and brightly painted furniture made a room look warmer and inviting.

Around 1820, candles began to be manufactured in Upper Canada. Before that they were imported, and very expensive.

One method of candle making involved dipping wicks over and over into hot tallow. Each time, the wicks were removed and the accumulated tallow was allowed to cool before re-dipping.

Most people made their own using melted fat, called tallow, while the wealthy used lamps that burned whale oil or lard. Kerosene and gas lamps came into greater use after 1841.

Pioneer Food

If you arrived when a family was eating a meal, you would be invited to join them. If the family was poor or if they were recent immigrants, you might eat from home-made wooden plates or bowls. Some immigrants brought dishes, cutlery, and pots with them. Others bought what they could not make from local craftsmen. If settlers could afford it, they bought dishes imported from Britain and the United States.

The foods eaten most were bread, potatoes, pork, and corn. Everything was prepared at home. Bread was made from corn, rye, and wheat flours, as were cakes and biscuits. Porridge, made from cornmeal, might be served for breakfast along with maple sugar. But often breakfast consisted of fried beef or pork, biscuits or bread, butter, and tea or cider or beer. If a farm had cows and poultry, milk, cheese, and eggs were enjoyed. Occasionally, there would be fish or chicken for a meal. In summer, on a farm, everyone worked an hour or more after dawn before eating breakfast.

The times of meals were not very different than they are today. Lunch, or dinner, was at noon; supper might be around 6 p.m. Poor families might eat only one or two meals a day consisting of potatoes and bread. While there were inns and taverns where travellers could eat, families did not go to them for meals. People ate at home.

What other foods were available? Pumpkins, cucumbers, beans, cabbages, and other vegetables were eaten fresh in season and pickled for use during the rest of the year. Pies were made with wild strawberries, raspberries, and other fruit. The further away from towns people were, the more fish and game (wild animals) they ate. Fresh meat and fish could be bought all year by those who could afford it, but most people ate fresh meat only in the summer. During the rest of the year, they ate salted or

Winnowing, or separating grain from the chaff, was done in the barn. The doors were left open to create a draft, and the mixture of chaff and grain was tossed into the air from a blanket. The wind blew the lighter chaff away.

smoked meat, vegetables that kept in storage, pickled vegetables, and dried fruit. Dried fruit was used to make pies, jams, jellies, apple sauce and apple cider. Real tea and coffee were expensive, so people created substitutes. They made teas from sassafras roots, hemlock sprigs and other plants. Coffee was made by roasting beans, corn, rye, wheat, or even dandelion roots. Mrs. Susanna Moodie describes the process:

> I carefully washed the roots quite clean, without depriving them of the fine brown skin which covers them and which contains the aromatic flavour which so nearly resembles coffee ... I cut my roots into small pieces the size of a kidney-bean, and roasted them on an iron baking-pan in the stove-oven until they were as brown and crisp as coffee. I then ground and transferred a small cupful of the powder to the coffee-pot, pouring upon it scalding water, and boiling it for a few minutes briskly over the fire ... The coffee proved excellent — far superior to the common coffee we procured at the stores.

Upper Canadians liked to eat heartily, and they liked variety

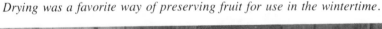

Drying was a favorite way of preserving fruit for use in the wintertime.

in their foods. They had many methods of preparing foods and of preserving those that would not keep fresh. But to eat well required many hours of hard work.

Household Tasks

Everyone in the family contributed to providing and preparing food. The men and boys were responsible for planting, cultivating and harvesting. Sometimes women and girls worked in the fields, but usually their tasks kept them in or around the house. Preparation of meat and bread took hours of work.

Most people did not live near markets, and even if they did, food was more expensive there. On a farm, men would butcher livestock and pack the meat into casks or barrels with dry salt or salt water, called brine, to preserve it. Or else meat would be smoked. Women and children might help or they would make lard or tallow from the fat. No part of a slaughtered animal was wasted. Liverwurst was made from the liver, headcheese from the head, and sausages from internal parts. Gelatine, made by boiling bone and cartilage, was used for jelly.

Tallow was used to make candles. The tallow was heated, and either candle wicks were dipped into it or it was poured into candle moulds. This was tricky work. The tallow had to be a precise temperature, and it had to cool at the right rate, or else the candles would crack or not burn properly.

To make bread, grain first had to be ground into flour. This could be done by crushing the grain with a stone or a wooden pounder or by grinding it between two round stones called grindstones. This was hard, time-consuming work. Settlers were relieved of this labor as more and more grist mills were built.

Baking was done at home in an outside oven or in a big iron kettle with a lid. When they could afford it, settlers built an oven beside the fireplace. It was heated by the fireplace, was more convenient, and eliminated the need for an extra fire. Even the yeast for bread and other baked products was made at home. It was produced by mixing boiled hops with flour. In large families, bread had to be baked almost every day. Pies, cakes, and biscuits were made less often.

All this cooking required a constant fire. Firewood had to be cut, split, and stacked. It had to be brought inside daily, and the ashes from the fireplace or stove had to be cleaned out. The smoke and ashes of wood fires caused a great deal of mess that required frequent cleaning.

Another important task that took a lot of time was making cloth and clothing. If pioneers could not afford to buy cloth, they made it from flax or wool. Flax was used to make linen. Women made sheets and tablecloths from fine linen cloth and work clothes, bags, and ropes from coarse linen.

After a farmer sheared the wool from a sheep, it had to be cleaned and prepared for spinning. Women and girls spent hours spinning, dyeing, and weaving. Then a family might hold a fulling bee. The wet cloth was laid out on a table. People sat all around

If there was no grist mill in the area, this type of hand-operated millstone might be used to grind grain into flour. The flour worked its way out through the furrows cut in the stone.

the table, and together they pushed and pulled on the cloth for several hours to make it shorter, thicker and stronger.

Women usually made clothes for everyone in the family. All sewing was done by hand because sewing machines had not been invented. Often a woman had one fine dress and a man had one well-tailored suit. These good clothes were worn on special occasions only and were kept for many years. Other clothes were mended and patched as long as possible. When they could no longer be used as clothes, they were cut into strips and woven into rugs. Nothing that had taken so much time and effort to make would be wasted.

Women usually did not have patterns from which to make clothes. They would copy an old garment, work from a picture, or create a design as they worked. A tailor would occasionally travel from town to town, staying in someone's home while he made clothes. Gradually, dressmakers and tailors set up shops in most communities. They relieved women of some of their sewing and tailoring tasks. People with money could buy cloth and clothing in town shops. Some of these products were made in Upper Canada while others were imported. Only wealthy people could buy new clothing frequently and keep up with changing styles.

The wealthy could also pay to have others wash and iron their clothes. In most families, however, the women and girls did these jobs by hand in a tub or by a stream bank.

Household tasks took a lot of time. In addition to the ones described, there were many others, such as butter-making, soap-making, quilting, cheese-making, and perhaps the brewing of beer. As well, there were the daily chores of cleaning and tidying. Upper Canada was considered a pioneer society as long as people had to produce all their own food and make most of the necessities of life.

The Family

Parents were responsible for the welfare and education of their children. Fathers taught their sons farming and trades. Mothers taught their daughters the numerous skills of homemaking.

Buying cloth was often impossible for pioneers and most women had to spend many hours weaving.

Parents often taught their children to read and write, for there were few schools in the early days, especially in the backwoods. This was usually the task of the mother rather than the father. A well-educated person might teach neighbors' children as well.

Men and women, boys and girls, had many distinct and different roles. An adult man was expected to support his family by farming or by going out to a job. A married woman was expected to have children, to look after their development, and to tend the house. Boys followed their fathers and girls their mothers. Large families were frequent in Upper Canada, one reason being the need for plenty of help around the home. Elizabeth Russell, who lived in York, wrote in 1811: "The women in this country are in general very prolific. I am intimately acquainted with a lady who lives in this place that has five pairs of twins four pairs of which are now living also two more children that she has had in single births — and has buried several besides. I think it is sixteen she has had in all. And she is now only about seven and thirty years of age . . . They marry very young here many girls not more than 13 or 14 years old."

Yet, while men and women had different roles, they also worked together on many tasks on the farm and at home. In other words, families did many things as a unit.

As well as working together, a family provided much of its own entertainment during its few hours of free time. In the evening, a family might spend time talking, reading, or singing together. Wealthier people often played card games and held dances accompanied by large dinners.

In winter, the family might go skating on a nearby lake or river, or sleigh-riding in the hills. In the summer, if they had any free time, they might go on a picnic.

Pioneers did not have much time for socializing, but neighbors did get together for bees to accomplish some task that needed co-operation. Bees were held to chop trees, burn the logs, build cabins, barns, mills, and harvest crops. After the land was settled, bees were held for all kinds of other purposes. There were quilting, sewing, pumpkin-slicing, fence-building, and house-warming bees. One kind of bee popular with the boys and girls was a corn-husking bee. Every time a boy found a red ear of corn, he could kiss the girl next to him.

But bees could be a lot of work for the hosts because they had to provide plenty of food and drink for the workers. Often, when the work was finished, a dance would end the bee. Bees were one of the few ways pioneers could break the isolation of their daily lives and, briefly, enjoy the company of other settlers. Weddings were also an occasion for celebration and partying.

Because pioneer families had little spare time and money, their pleasures and entertainments were simple. The family was much more the centre of both work and play than it is today.

Life in the Towns and Cities

Even before 1791, Upper Canada had urban centres. An urban centre might be a hamlet, village, town, or city, depending on its size. Hamlets and villages had a few hundred people and were the smallest. Towns had a few thousand inhabitants, while cities had the largest population. Towns and cities had more control over their own governments than smaller communities did.

The Growth of Towns

As the Loyalists settled along the St. Lawrence River and Lake Ontario, they founded communities such as Cornwall, Brockville, Gananoque, Kingston, Ernestown (now called Bath), Napanee, and Belleville. Government assistance often aided the building and growth of these communities.

Kingston

Kingston developed as a British military and naval base for Lake Ontario. The government bought large quantities of food and building supplies from around Upper Canada. Local people found jobs working for the troops, in the shipyard, and on fortifications. For the first forty years of Upper Canada's history, Kingston was the largest and most important urban centre. But the military and naval base was only part of the reason. Kingston also benefited from an advantageous geographical location.

Goods from Montreal were shipped up the St. Lawrence River to Lake Ontario and on to fur-trading posts in the West. When these goods reached Lake Ontario, they were put on

Kingston, seen here from Fort Henry in 1828, was for many years Upper Canada's largest and most important urban centre.

sailing vessels. Kingston's large harbor was the best place for this transhipment. Later, goods from the West and from Upper Canada going downriver were also transhipped at Kingston. As the harbor was used more and more, other related services became necessary. Because goods often had to be stored at Kingston before they could be put on a ship, warehouses were needed, as were merchants to manage these warehouses and supply the ships. In this way, more businesses developed to serve the active harbor.

Kingston also benefited from the early settlement of surrounding farmland. Gradually a village formed to provide services for residents. In 1785, a school was opened; a post office followed in 1789. Kingston's population was larger than that of any other urban centre in the province. Its merchants sold goods all over Upper Canada and, as early as 1808, a regular stagecoach route was established between it and Montreal. As a result of the economic growth of Kingston, the first banks in Upper Canada developed there.

In 1819, Kingston had twice-weekly steamship service to

the Bay of Quinte and a weekly steamer to York and Niagara. Kingston gained a water route to the Ottawa River when the Rideau Canal opened in 1832. But Kingston was accessible by land as well as by water, which added to its growth.

Between 1836 and 1839, the road from Kingston to Napanee was one of the first in Upper Canada to be *macadamized*. Macadamization was a method of paving roads using crushed stone, or gravel. Early Canadian roads had only a small amount of gravel in them, so the early macadamized roads were only slightly better than dirt roads.

Niagara

Niagara and York were also major urban centres. Their histories date back to the 1790s when Lieutenant Governor Simcoe chose Niagara (renamed Newark, now Niagara-on-the-Lake) as the first capital of the province. Niagara continued to be important even after the capital was moved because it was at one end of an important trade route.

Niagara Falls, on the Niagara River, prevented ships from sailing between Lakes Ontario and Erie. Goods had to be carried overland around the Falls and reloaded on sailing ships. Military supplies and goods for the fur trade went up the Niagara River to Lake Erie; furs and later farm products came down.

Immigrants travelling westward took the portage route around Niagara Falls. Along with Niagara, Queenstown (Queenston), Chippewa (Chippawa), and Fort Erie were all on this early trade route. They all developed to serve the needs of traders and immigrants.

Niagara benefited from the establishment of Fort George (1796), the major British military base at the western end of Lake Ontario. Similarly, Fort Erie's growth was stimulated by the British military base on Lake Erie.

Niagara became the capital of the Niagara District in 1800. Officials met here to decide matters of local importance, such as the building of roads, court houses, and jails. These officials established fire regulations, appointed constables (policemen), regulated markets, controlled the sale of liquor, and determined the right of the clergy to perform marriages. As Niagara's population increased, services developed and the number of churches, newspapers, libraries, doctors, and lawyers grew. For many years Niagara remained the most important town on the Niagara Peninsula.

York (Toronto)

Lieutenant Governor Simcoe originally planned to establish Upper Canada's capital at the forks of the Thames River, where London now stands. The site was in the middle of the wilderness, and it would take years to build roads from there to the shores of Lakes Ontario and Erie. In the meantime, Simcoe decided to use York as an interim capital. He felt that York was safer than Niagara, which was right on the American border. York, which is now Toronto, has remained the capital of the province ever since.

In the summer of 1793, the Queen's Rangers began clearing land at York to build a British fort. Soon officials and their families moved from Niagara. York had an excellent harbor, the Don and Humber Rivers, and roads. Simcoe stressed road building.

By 1796, Yonge Street was opened. It ran from York to Lake Simcoe. Dundas Road ran from Burlington Bay, at the head of Lake Ontario, to the forks of the Thames. By 1800, Dundas Road was extended to York, which already had Danforth Road running to Kingston. York had become the centre of Upper Canada's first road network.

But these roads, which still exist today, were not as we know them now. They were unpaved, littered with tree stumps, and obstructed by rivers. Travel on them was not easy, but they were better than no roads at all. They helped to open the area around York to settlement, especially along Yonge Street. Improvements in road construction began around 1830. Part of Yonge Street was macadamized, and part of Danforth, or Kingston Road, was paved with planks.

York's first inhabitants were troops and government officials. But it was not long before the village began attracting

York grew rapidly in the 1830s. This scene of King St. West was painted in 1838, four years after the city was incorporated as the City of Toronto.

merchants, skilled tradespeople, and unskilled workers. Tradespeople and laborers found work in shops, mills, construction, industry, and in services. By 1812, York had many industries: potasheries, where potash was made from ashes; tanneries, where leather was made from animal skins; breweries, brickyards, a shipbuilding yard, and a pottery factory. The development of commercial industries was followed by the development of service industries. The town began providing tailors, hairdressers, watchmakers, bakers, teachers, doctors, and lawyers to meet the villagers' needs. York's growth was also helped by rich surrounding farmlands.

The building of canals in the 1820s helped to make York the trading centre for the surrounding area and areas to the west. The Erie Canal was built connecting Lake Erie, at Buffalo, to New York City. In 1828, it was joined to Lake Ontario by a canal at Oswego, New York. This gave York a water route with access to the Atlantic Ocean as an alternative to the St. Lawrence River. Merchants could now buy directly from European or American sources, which was cheaper than buying through merchants in Montreal and Kingston. York's trade with the West was helped in 1829 by the opening of the Welland Canal which joined Lakes Ontario and Erie. As York's trade grew, Kingston's transhipment trade declined.

The area around York was called the Home District. York was the capital of this district. With the great increase in immigration in the 1830s, York and the Home District grew rapidly. The town's population increased from 2,860 in 1830 to 9,700 in 1834. York was overtaking Kingston as the main urban centre of Upper Canada. In 1834, it was renamed and became the City of Toronto.

Smaller Urban Centres

The urban centres of western Upper Canada developed slowly. Simcoe's attempt to create a naval base, shipbuilding centre, and local capital at Chatham on the Thames River did not succeed. According to a traveller who passed through Chatham in 1820, the town had "only one house and a sort of church." Over the next ten years, it developed slowly into a village. By the 1830s, Chatham was a market centre for local farmers. But despite this growth and the fact that many immigrants passed through the village, few chose to stay.

Other government efforts to establish urban centres at the western end of the province were more successful. In 1796, the British built a military base at Amherstburg. Fort Malden was the naval base for Lakes Erie and Huron. In the same year, the government built a court house and offices at Sandwich to encourage settlement. These two centres, on the banks of the Detroit River, were on the trade route between Lake Erie and the upper lakes.

Early urban centres usually developed where there was a harbor, or along rivers and canals where there was water power to run mills. They often had good farmland around them, which attracted farmers and merchants and created the need for a

Guelph in 1830. The town was founded in 1827 by John Galt, who struck the first axe-blow to the maple tree which had been chosen as the town site. The stump is seen in the foreground. A flag flies over the town market building.

market centre. Government support could be significant to a centre's growth. For example, London grew as a market centre for the local farmers, but it did not become an important community until the government chose it as a district capital in 1826. Then, its population grew rapidly. Its importance further increased when the British government decided to put a garrison there. In 1840, London officially became a village.

Thomas Need owned a sawmill which was the starting point for Bobcaygeon. Here is his account of how many communities began:

> The erection of a saw mill is always the first marked event in the formation of a settlement in the bush. At first, some one or two adventurers ... purchase a few acres of land on the bank of a river or stream, where ... there is good water power; two or three rude huts or shanties are erected, and a small clearing made in the forest ... others are

attracted to the spot; the original settler [makes money and uses it to build a saw mill] ... this induces many to come into the neighbourhood, from the facility it offers for building. Then, as the settlement increases, some bold man is persuaded to erect a grist or flour mill, which again serves as an attraction; a growing population requires the necessaries of life at hand; stores are opened, a tavern licensed, and in a few years a thriving village, or, as in the case of Peterboro', an important town, springs up in the heart of the forest.

Bytown (Ottawa)

The British government feared that, in the event of another war with the United States, the Americans could easily cut the route along the St. Lawrence between Montreal and Kingston. They decided that a second, safer route to Kingston was necessary. As a result, between 1826 and 1832, the Rideau Canal was built. The project took six years. It was a tremendous undertaking requiring forty-seven stone locks as well as walls on the canal and roads. Thousands of workers had to be brought in along with great quantities of supplies. The canal joined the Ottawa River between the Chaudière and Rideau Falls. Bridges were built across the Ottawa River to Hull. There had been some early settlement at Hull and along the Ottawa Valley shortly after 1800. But it was the building of the Rideau Canal that really gave these settlements their start.

As construction of the canal continued, wharves, storehouses, government offices, and homes for the workers were erected. Bytown sprang into existence. It was named after the man in charge of the canal project, Colonel John By. Soon the village had taverns, churches, and a volunteer fire department. Its population grew from scarcely any people in 1826 to about 1,500 in 1832. It continued to grow in the years following and served the needs of lumbermen and farmers of the area. In 1855, the name of Bytown was changed to Ottawa, and in 1857, Ottawa was made capital of the Province of Canada.

Bytown in 1835, as seen from present-day Parliament Hill. The town was named after Colonel John By, who supervised the building of the Rideau Canal. In 1855, its name was changed to Ottawa.

Living in a Town

If you live in a city or a village today, you expect to have paved streets, sidewalks, street lights, sewers to take away rain water and waste, pure water piped to your house, electricity, and often gas or oil for heat. You expect to have garbage collection as well as fire and police protection. Can you imagine a town with none of these things? You would not have found these services in the villages of early Upper Canada.

The unpaved streets turned to mud in the rain and produced clouds of dust when they were dry. By the 1830s, a few main streets were macadamized or planked, but most remained unpaved. Sidewalks were also occasionally laid with planks. Most often, however, streets and sidewalks were not maintained. Holes appeared in streets; rotten or loose planks could make sidewalks dangerous. Sometimes people caused further problems. For example, according to a complaint of April, 1800, the streets of York were "frequently obstructed and made dangerous to passengers, by piles of wood and stones placed in them as well as by pits dug in several places." Even though the streets were in poor condition, there were wagon drivers who drove fast and without regard for the safety of people.

Because towns had no regular garbage collection, people did what they liked with refuse. They threw it onto roads or into streams and lakes. Garbage piled on the ice in winter would be carried away by the spring thaw. A complaint of 1832 refers to York's harbor: "All the filth of the town — dead horses, dogs, cats, manure, etc. heaped up together on the ice, to drop down, in a few days into the water ... If they have no regard for the health of their fellow-beings, are they not afraid to poison the fish that supply their own tables?" Many people got their water for drinking and washing from the same lakes and rivers into which they threw their garbage, although there were other sources of household water such as wells and rain barrels that caught water running off the roof. Waste water ran away in ditches to swamps, lakes and rivers.

Cholera was one of the most dreaded diseases of the time. It usually broke out among steerage passengers on immigrant ships and its spread was rapid. Epidemics raged through Upper Canada in 1832 and 1834, killing thousands.

CHOLERA BULLETIN.

Printed at the Wesleyan Office.

TO the President of the Board of Health of the Gore District:

*Sir----*I have this morning received a communication from Doct. GILPIN of Brantford, stating he was called to visit Three cases, which he considers exhibited characters of Spasmodic Cholera. One case, a man by the name of **Young**, proved fatal in **8** hours. The other two were convalescent when Doctor Gilpin writes.

The following is a report I submit to the Board of Health, on the above cases:

Cases of CHOLERA in the Gore District, from June **23**, *to June* **25**, *inclusive----*

Brantford, Cases **THREE**, Deaths **1**, Convalescent **2**.

(Signed)   **SLADE ROBINSON,**
Hamilton, June **27, 1832.**   Pres't Medical Board.

In pioneer Upper Canada, it was a lucky town that had a hand-operated fire engine which could be pulled by horses or men to the scene of a fire.

In spite of complaints about the dirt and smell of garbage, and even though people knew that garbage and polluted water were unhealthy, little was done to improve the situation. Then in 1832 there was a cholera epidemic. Illness spread up the St. Lawrence throughout Upper Canada. While the exact number is not known, there were thousands of deaths. Because it was known that cholera can be caused by dirt, town governments began garbage collection and installed a few sewage drains. But this effort was not kept up.

People had, however, become more concerned about proper drainage, garbage disposal, and pure water. And while it took almost ten years to raise the money and do the work, by 1841 Toronto had a water system. It used wooden pipes and brought water from the lake. Other cities and towns soon began to acquire water systems.

The main purpose of these water systems, however, was not to provide clean water for people but to make sure that there was water available to fight fires. In those days, towns did not have hydrants and fire departments with people and equipment ready to move as soon as they heard the signal. Fire was a serious threat to early towns. Many houses were wooden and had poorly constructed or open fireplaces. Fire fighting was done by the townspeople. Every house was required to have a water bucket and a ladder on the roof near the chimney. When a fire broke out, everyone rushed to it with their buckets. The citizens were lucky if the town had a fire engine, with a tank, pump, and hoses mounted on wheels, that could be pulled by men or horses to the fire. The fire engine was much more efficient than a line of people passing and throwing buckets of water on the fire. If a fire was large, it was unlikely that these bucket brigades could put it out.

In the 1820s and 1830s towns began to establish volunteer fire departments. The volunteers worked without pay. When the fire bell rang, they left their work, hurried to get the engine, and rushed to the scene of the fire. By the time they arrived, the fire could have done a lot of damage. The problems of adequate water supply and effective means of fighting fires remained long after 1841.

Also, towns did not have full-time police forces. A town's chief of police was called a high constable or high bailiff and constables were appointed from among the citizens. Appoint-

Dundurn Castle as it stands today in Hamilton. It was built in 1832, and the original brick was later covered with stucco.

The people of Upper Canada had to provide their own entertainment. In winter, skating and sleigh-riding were favorite forms of amusement.

ments were not by choice; if a person did not want to serve he had to pay a fine. The constables were not paid and were not armed. They had to patrol the streets and make arrests. Streets were not well lit, and patrolling in winter could be very unpleasant. Towns without constables sometimes hired a night-watch who patrolled at night, watching for fires or any trouble. He also called out the time and the weather conditions.

As villages grew into towns, there was evidence of both wealth and poverty. People with money had carriages and fine clothes and lived in large houses of brick, stone, or wood.

Good building stone was only available in a few places, and was too heavy to transport long distances. Clay, to make bricks, was found in many parts of Upper Canada, and bricks were not difficult to transport. Yet, it was not until the 1830s that brick was widely used for homes. In the 1840s, brickyards began manufacturing both red and yellow bricks. Even though they were more expensive, yellow bricks were more popular than red ones.

There are some examples of early brick houses still standing in Upper Canada: the Grange and the Campbell house in Toronto; Belle Vue in Amherstburg; and Dundurn Castle, which has stucco over the brick, in Hamilton. You can also see stone houses dating from this time: Homewood near Maitland on the St. Lawrence, and H.K. Pinhey's house "Horaceville" on the Ottawa River.

But most city-dwellers were not wealthy. There were large numbers of tradespeople and shopkeepers, who formed the middle class, and ever-increasing numbers of poor.

Cities often attract the poor because of the opportunities they provide. Immigrants who were unable to establish themselves in a new country, families whose means of support was lost through war or illness, and children who were left homeless for the same reasons were all a part of the growing poor. By the 1830s, Toronto already had areas of poor housing, called slums. They originally centred around the city's two rivers.

Still, Upper Canadian cities were often better than many European and American cities. They were smaller, and their problems of dirt, disease, and poverty were not quite as severe.

As the towns and cities of Upper Canada grew in population, so did their social facilities. While most people amused themselves at home, there was plenty to do and see in towns. There were horse races and travelling circuses. If there was a garrison in the town, the troops would march on special occasions. And of course there were skating and sleigh-riding in the winter.

The Growth of Upper Canada

By 1841, Upper Canadians had created a flourishing agricultural society. In many ways, it had passed beyond the pioneer stage. Farming areas along the lakeshores and on the Niagara Peninsula were developing features of a mature society: villages and towns which served farmers' needs, mills, roads, and regular stage-coach service carrying passengers and mail. Farm machinery, agricultural societies, and big new homes and barns were also indicators of maturity. Communities like Toronto, Kingston, and Niagara were no longer small settlements on the edge of the forest. They were busy urban centres whose merchants dealt with such distant cities as London, England, and New York. There were schools, hospitals, libraries, banks, insurance companies, newspapers, and a variety of manufacturing establishments. Upper Canadian ports were linked by rivers, lakes, and a network of canals, and there were plans to build railways.

Despite these advances, large areas of the province still existed at a pioneer level. A few miles inland from the Great Lakes, thick forests still covered much of Upper Canada. Stumps littered farmers' fields, and settlers still lived in log cabins with home-made furniture, food, and clothing. In these areas, there were few schools or churches, and farms and villages were linked by poor roads that could not be used many months of the year. But, just as the older settled areas had progressed from this level, so would the backwoods.

In another sense, Upper Canada was still an undeveloped society. It was very dependent on the outside world, Britain in

As the number of settlers in an area increased, a blacksmith would set up shop in the village. In addition to shoeing horses, he fitted iron rims to wagon wheels and made cooking utensils and a variety of other items.

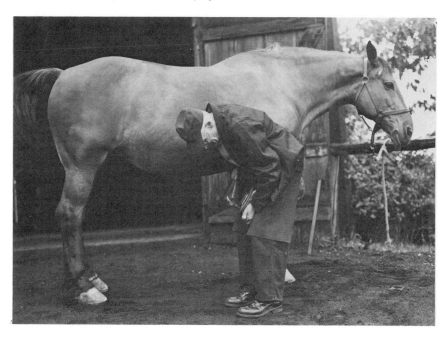

Early pioneers made their own brooms, but as an area became more settled, a broommaker would probably arrive with his machine and set up shop.

particular. From London came political direction as well as general supervision over the provincial government. The prosperity of Upper Canadian farmers and merchants was dependent upon markets and traders in Europe and the United States. Money for business ventures and public works projects, such as the Welland Canal, had to be borrowed from outside the province.

Upper Canada also depended upon other countries for people. Immigrants from the United States and, after 1815, from Britain and Europe, expanded settlement and towns. The needs of new settlers created jobs and business opportunities. Without immigration, Upper Canada would have remained a small, struggling settlement.

Dependence on other nations existed for pioneer communities all over North America. This dependence would continue for Upper Canada, and for the rest of British North America, long after 1841. But the foundation for the development of the province of Ontario had been laid. Upper Canada was firmly established as an attractive home for immigrants, whose arrival would enrich Ontario with a large and varied population. Urbanization, or the growth of cities, was off to a strong start. Ontario's future as a major food producer was ensured as farming technology improved. And with the building of railways, industrial growth would be further stimulated.

The same sort of development can be seen in the province's

When a grist mill opened, farmers brought their grain for grinding from many miles away.

social life. Beginnings were made in education, religious organization, and health care which would mature after 1841.

Religion and Churches

The Christian religion and church attendance were important in Upper Canadian society. Most people were Christian and looked to a church to satisfy many needs. But in pioneer societies it was often difficult to organize settlers into a church congregation. Backwoods settlers were too few and far between, or too poor, to support a church. Whenever a clergyman was available, he would hold services in homes, barns, and even taverns. But pioneers spent so much time and energy meeting their most basic needs that it was not easy for them to attend religious services. The first problem churches in Upper Canada faced was the need to reach the people.

In the early days, the Methodist Church was the most successful in meeting the desire of the pioneers for religious services. *Circuit riders*, or ministers who travelled through the backwoods, held meetings wherever people could gather. These ministers were carefully trained by practical apprenticeship in the United States. They knew how to speak to settlers in simple language and appeal to their basic emotions. The Methodists succeeded in reaching thousands of pioneers who were not being served by any other church. The numbers of Methodists grew rapidly, and at one time they may have been the largest religious group in Upper Canada.

Other large religious groups were Presbyterians, Anglicans, Baptists, and Roman Catholics. There were also many smaller groups, such as Mennonites and Quakers. All these denominations were allowed to worship freely. Ontario's religious diversity and freedom were established early in its history.

That does not mean, however, that there were no problems involving religion. There were often disagreements between and within religious groups. There were arguments about an established church, about the government's relationship to churches, and about the place of religion in schools.

An established church is one that is supported by the government and has a prominent position in society. It is supported by the government with money and land, and it, in turn, may influence the laws the government makes. An established church usually has some control over education. The Anglican Church, which was established in Britain, claimed the same position in Upper Canada. All other churches disagreed. While they were technically correct, the Anglican Church did have special privileges. For example, it received most of the benefits from the sale and lease of Clergy Reserves. Government officials, from the lieutenant governor down, regularly favored the Anglican Church in its claims to lands, revenue, and influence. This support was strengthened by John Strachan's presence on the Executive and Legislative Councils. He argued that the Anglican Church should receive all the benefits from the Reserves. He also wanted church control of schools from elementary to university level.

The issue of an established church had political as well as religious significance. The Anglican Church supported the Family Compact while the other churches supported the reformers. Church privilege became an issue in elections. Newspapers took

The British Whig,

AND GENERAL ADVRTISER FOR THE MIDLAND DISTRICT.

VOL. VI.   KINGSTON, U. C. SATURDAY, APRIL 8th, 1837.   No. 13.

ter the usual compliments, the following conversation ensued:—

"Governor. Well, Hutbuck, how did you like the candles?

"Indian. Berry well.

"Governor. Did you burn them all yet?

"Indian.—Burn him! I eat him.

"Governor. You ate them?

"Indian. Yes, I boil him with my corn, and eat him all up.

"Governor. And how did they eat?

"Indian. Why, the *fruit* eat berry well, but the *core* stick in my squaw *trote*, and nearly choke him—that's all."

RICHARD CARLISLE A CHRISTIAN.— We copy the following from the police report of the London Morning Herald, Feb. 6th.

Mr. Richard Carlisle, who for many years past sustained an unenviable notoriety as a vender of deistical and blasphemous publications, presented himself before Mr. Alderman T. Wood, to attest his conviction of the truth of Christianity. He produced a set of declarations, such as are taken by dissenting ministers, as preliminary to other necessary steps to becoming a legal teacher of a congregation. He was desired to read his declarations aloud, which he did, in a decorous and apparently sincere manner.

The first was a declaration of fidelity to the King, and of abhorrence of certain popish tenets. Then followed a profession of faith:—"I, Richard Carlisle, profess faith in God the Father, and Jesus Christ, his eternal Son, the true God; and in the Holy Spirit—one God, blessed evermore. And do acknowledge the holy scriptures of the Old and New Testament to be given by Divine inspiration. The next was that he preferred the Protestant to the Roman Catholic version of the Bible. "I, Richard Carlile, do solemnly declare, in the presence of Almighty God, that I am a Christian and a Protestant, and as such that I believe that the scriptures of the Old and New Testament, as commonly received among protestant churches, do contain the revealed will of God, and that I do receive the same as the rule of my doctrine and practice."

Daily newspapers first made their appearance in the 1830s. Kingston's British Whig, *today the* Whig-Standard, *is Canada's oldest continuous daily.*

Bishop John Strachan was a major figure in the political, religious, and educational life of Upper Canada.

sides and filled their pages with statements by church leaders.

Perhaps the paper most widely read was the *Christian Guardian*. It was begun in 1829 by the Methodist Church with Egerton Ryerson as editor. Ryerson urged the government "to do away with all political distinctions on account of religious faith — to remove all ministers of religion from seats and places of political power in the Provincial Government — to grant to the Clergy of all denominations . . . the enjoyment of equal rights and privileges . . . to appropriate the proceeds of the sale of lands heretofore set apart for the support of a Protestant Clergy, to the purposes of general education and various internal improvements." In short, he wanted separation of church and state.

In the 1820s and 1830s, the provincial government made plans to share the proceeds of the Clergy Reserves, and different churches began to receive small amounts of government support. In 1831, the Catholic bishop, Alexander Macdonell, became a member of the Legislative Council. But the Anglican Church still had special privileges, and the conflict over this continued for a long time.

The clergy was involved with schools from the early days when teachers were Anglican ministers. Later, a few Methodist and Baptist ministers were hired. Churches established their own schools. In 1837, the Methodists opened Upper Canada Academy in Cobourg, renaming it Victoria College in 1841. The Roman Catholics established Regiopolis College and the Presbyterians prepared to open Queen's University. Bishop Strachan wanted to create a provincial university under Anglican control. In 1827, he received a royal charter from Britain for King's College. But there was much opposition to Strachan's plans in both Britain and Upper Canada. This delayed the opening of King's College and the beginning of a university until after 1841.

Through Sunday Schools, churches provided children with basic education in reading and writing as well as in religious doctrines. The Catholic Church sought to have its own schools, with priests as teachers. The issue of separate schools — schools run by churches separately from government supported schools —developed after 1841. The problem of government support for separate schools still exists in Ontario.

The Churches and Social Problems

In spite of the influence of religion, the clergy found much to criticize in the behavior of Upper Canadians. People drank, fought, swore, and disregarded the churches' teachings. The clergy tried to change people's behavior by persuasion and, eventually, by government action.

One of the major issues churches campaigned against was excessive drinking of alcohol. Whisky, hard cider, and beer were produced in large quantities all over Upper Canada. Whisky was made inexpensively from spoiled or poor quality grain which could not be used to make flour. As more grist mills were built to meet farmers' needs, so were more distilleries built to make whisky. Alcoholic beverages were drunk by men, women, and children of all classes, at home and in public. People believed whisky stimulated their energies and might also prevent colds. Whisky was drunk whenever settlers got together at meetings, elections, weddings, funerals, and bees. Elections and bees seem to have been the occasions when the heaviest drinking and the worst disorders took place.

The clergy believed that excessive drinking caused crime, poverty, death, and disorder. The Methodist, Baptist, and Presbyterian leaders' campaign against drinking was called the temperance movement. Some temperance leaders wanted people to drink moderately while others called for abstinence, that is no drinking at all.

The temperance movement existed earlier in the United States and in Lower Canada. There was some American influence, therefore, in the movement's growth in Upper Canada in the 1820s. This caused some people, particularly Anglican clergymen and political conservatives, to be suspicious of the movement. The first Upper Canadian temperance society was formed in 1828, and by 1832 membership numbered about one hundred. Such societies required their members to pledge themselves to drink moderately or to totally abstain. They tried to discourage settlers from serving alcohol at bees and at other social functions. In the 1830s, temperance societies asked the government to pass laws to restrain the manufacture and sale of liquor. No significant restrictive laws were made before 1841, but the idea of using the law to control liquor was accepted by temperance supporters. This campaign would be pushed further in the 1840s and later.

Before 1841 some churches had also begun a campaign to restrict people's activities on Sundays. For example, in 1833, Thomas Radcliffe wrote about a clergyman who successfully petitioned to have Sunday fishing prohibited. In later years, laws prohibiting business and many other activities on Sunday would be extended. Few of these laws exist today, but some were changed only recently.

Schools

Children in Upper Canada were not required by law to attend school. Those who were lucky enough to be educated did not attend well-equipped schools, with trained teachers, all paid for by taxes. The system of education that exists today was barely started before 1841.

The earliest schools were run by people who charged fees

A village might have a school, but the children probably had no note-books or texts.

and taught in their homes. These schoolmasters advertised to attract pupils.

Pupils were usually required to bring firewood with them to help heat the classroom, and candles if school was held at night. Teachers did not have to be trained or licensed as they do today. Nor were children required to pass certain courses. Reading, writing, English grammar, arithmetic, and religion were the most frequently taught subjects, with Latin and Greek sometimes added.

This kind of education was not practical, but then these schools were not intended to serve the needs of children in the backwoods. Practical education or training in a trade was done by apprenticeship. A boy worked alongside a tradesman and learned by watching and doing.

An exception to the usual sort of schoolmaster was John Strachan. From 1803 to 1812, Strachan ran his own school in Cornwall. There he taught practical arithmetic and natural science along with the usual subjects. He set high academic standards for his pupils, and used rewards and competition, rather than force, to maintain discipline. His school closed when he moved to York in 1812, but he was recognized as one of the best teachers in Upper Canada.

A public system, partly financed by government funds and partly by pupils' parents, was started in 1807. A grammar school, somewhat like our high school, was provided in each district.

A typical advertisement for a privately-run school.

But these schools served few children. They were located in towns and charged board and tuition fees which not many people could afford. Strachan proposed a provincial school system, financed and supervised by the government, with no fees charged to poor students. He had many supporters.

More schools were needed outside of towns and at lower cost to parents. In 1816, the Common School Act achieved this. Although parents still had to pay fees, they were lower than those for grammar schools.

A typical common school was a log cabin with benches for the pupils and a desk for the teacher. Pupils still had to bring firewood in the winter for the stove or fireplace that heated the room. A pail of water was drawn from a well outside for drinking. The availability of books, paper, and pens depended on what parents could afford. Students usually wrote on slates which were used again and again. The teachers' books included a Bible, speller, grammar, reader, and an arithmetic book. Few teachers had history and geography books. Methods of teaching were very simple, and students were often required to memorize parts of books. Schools closed for the summer, and sometimes

These ads from the Constitution *of September 6, 1837 give some idea of people's preoccupations and of the goods and services that had become available in Upper Canada.*

for as long as six months, because children were needed to help on farms.

There were other types of schools in Upper Canada as well. Osgoode Hall was established to train lawyers, and a medical school was opened in York in 1832. Mechanics' Institutes were started to provide part-time education for adults. Educational facilities are an important part of a mature society. Upper Canada was beginning to develop facilities similar to those found in Britain and the United States.

Health and Medical Care

Upper Canada had few health or medical services. The first hospital opened in York in 1829, and by 1832 Kingston had a

Boats were the most important means of transportation in Upper Canada. Several types are seen here including, in the foreground, the Durham boat, a flat-bottomed craft used on rivers. It could be sailed or poled along the river bed.

hospital too. The York hospital was intended for the poor who could not afford the cost of doctor's care at home. Patients without money received free care while others were charged a small fee. Most towns and rural areas had a resident doctor, but that was all. There were few apothecaries, or druggists, and even fewer dentists.

Yet the need for medical care was great. It was difficult for people living in log cabins to keep warm and dry, especially in the winter. Many did not always get enough of the kinds of food that could help their bodies heal themselves. When a person suffered an injury, such as a severe cut or broken bone, he or she could not be rushed to a local hospital. It might be hours or days before a doctor could come to attend to the injured person. A vaccination against smallpox was known, but not all children received it. Vaccines to prevent measles, diphtheria, and other diseases were not available.

In most cases, Upper Canadians treated themselves at home

with herbs and traditional cures. The remedies pioneers used included tea made from the wormwood plant, tea made from hemlock or spearmint, May-apple roots, burdock roots, crushed plantain leaves, and the roots, leaves, fruit and bark of many other plants. Pioneers also learned to set bones and pull teeth.

A doctor's treatment was often the same as that which people provided themselves. Medical practices were still very crude. Doctors did not know about germs, and so they did not sterilize equipment before operating. One frequent remedy for illness was blood-letting, which meant allowing the patient to bleed. While whisky and opium were often given to relieve pain, many operations were performed while the patient was conscious. All doctors were handicapped by limited medical knowledge.

The care of the sick was yet another skill the pioneers had to have. Many years passed before Ontario had adequate medical and hospital services.

Upper Canada and the Future

In 1841, Upper Canada was on the threshold of great change. There was the new political connection with Lower Canada as established by the Union Act. From this Act would emerge an important problem: how would French-speaking and English-speaking Canadians live together? This problem is still with us today.

Economic life would change profoundly as railways were built, manufacturing industries grew, population increased, and trade with Britain and the United States expanded. These and other developments affected social life. Over the next two decades, the pioneer age in southern Upper Canada would pass into history.

Upper Canada was built by the hard work of thousands of pioneers. Their laws and values and the society they created still affect the way we live. Examples of what they built, some of their homes and tools, can still be seen and are worth preserving. They help us understand our past and what kind of people we are.

Selected Biographies

BRANT, Chief Joseph

Joseph Brant, whose Indian name was Thayendanegea, was born in Ohio in 1742. He was educated at a Protestant school in Connecticut, where he learned English and was converted to Christianity.

As principal chief of the Six Nation Indians, he was highly respected by his own people and by influential white people as well. During the American War of Independence, Brant fought on the side of the British. After the war, he led the Mohawk tribe to the valley of the Grand River, where he was given a large tract of land.

While continuing to rule over his people, Brant did missionary work, wrote several religious books, and translated into Mohawk parts of the Gospels and the Church of England prayer book. He died on the reservation in November 1807.

DUNLOP, William "Tiger"

Born in Scotland in 1792, William Dunlop first came to Canada as an army surgeon during the War of 1812. He later accompanied his regiment to India where he acquired his nickname "Tiger." Stories vary as to exactly how he earned it. Between 1820 and 1826 he lived in London and Edinburgh, teaching medicine and writing. In 1826, Dunlop returned to Canada in the service of the Canada Company. He helped clear the land where the city of Guelph now stands and founded Goderich, where he built his home. From 1841 to 1846, he was a member of the Legislative Assembly of Canada.

Capable and conscientious in his work, Dunlop was nevertheless one of the most colorful characters of his day. Stories about his practical jokes and eccentricities of dress and behavior abound. He was also a lively, witty writer and published many essays and two books. He never married and died near Lachine, Quebec, in 1848.

DURHAM, John George Lambton, 1st earl of

The son of a wealthy landowner, Durham was born in England in 1792. In 1813 he was elected to the House of Commons where his radical ideas earned him the nickname "Radical Jack." He became Baron Durham in 1828 and served as Lord Privy Seal from 1830 to 1833. From 1835 to 1837 he was British ambassador to Russia.

When the rebellions broke out in Upper and Lower Canada in 1837, Durham was appointed Governor-in-Chief and High Commissioner of British North America. On his arrival in Canada, he promptly set about investigating the causes of the discontent and taking such steps as he thought necessary to settle the trouble. Some of these steps, particularly the granting of amnesty to most of the French-Canadian rebels, were strongly criticized by the British Government. Durham resigned towards the end of 1838.

After his return to England, he prepared his famous *Report* which advocated uniting the two Canadas and granting the colony responsible government. Durham died in the summer of 1840.

MACKENZIE, William Lyon

William Lyon Mackenzie was born in Scotland in 1795. He came to Canada in 1820 and went into business as a shop-keeper. Politically active and outspoken, he soon founded a journal, the *Colonial Advocate*, through which he voiced his radical political philosophy and attacked the Family Compact, Upper Canada's ruling group.

In 1828, Mackenzie was elected to the Legislative Assembly. His sharp tongue got him expelled five times, but each time he was re-elected. In 1834 he was chosen Toronto's first mayor.

By 1837, Mackenzie had become bitter over his Reform party's failure to get changes made. He organized radical reformers, mostly farmers from north of Toronto, and staged a rebellion. It was, from the rebel's point of view, a disaster, and Mackenzie fled to the United States.

In 1849, Mackenzie was allowed to return to Canada. He was once again elected to the Assembly in 1851, but his influence was slight. He retired to private life in 1858 and died in Toronto in 1861.

MOODIE, Susanna

Born in Suffolk, England in 1803, Susanna Strickland married Lieutenant J.W.D. Moodie in 1831 and emigrated to Canada with him the following year. The Moodies originally settled near Cobourg. Two years later, they moved to a 400-acre farm north of Peterborough, where they found it very difficult to adjust to the hardships of pioneer life. In 1839, they thankfully escaped to Belleville where life was easier. They had seven children. After her husband's death in 1869, Mrs. Moodie moved to Toronto. She died there in 1885.

Susanna Moodie's career as an author began with a book of poems published in London in 1830. In 1847 she and her husband founded a literary magazine in Belleville. It survived for a year. The author of several novels and many sketches, stories, and poems, Susanna Moodie is best known for her book *Roughing it in the Bush*, in which she described with color and humor her experiences as a settler in the backwoods of Upper Canada.

ROBINSON, Peter

Peter Robinson was born in New Brunswick in 1785. He came to Upper Canada with his family in 1792 and settled first in Kingston and later in

York. In the War of 1812, he commanded a rifle company at the capture of Detroit.

In 1817, Robinson was elected to the Legislative Assembly of Upper Canada. In 1824 and 1825, he helped to settle large numbers of Irish immigrants in the area of Peterborough. The town was named after him. He was appointed commissioner of Crown lands, with a seat in the Executive and Legislative Councils, in 1827. In 1836, he resigned along with the entire Executive Council in a dispute with Sir Francis Bond Head. Robinson died in 1838.

RYERSON, Egerton

Egerton Ryerson was born in the township of Charlotteville in Upper Canada in 1803. He was the son of a United Empire Loyalist. After being educated at the district grammar school, he entered the Methodist ministry in 1825. In 1829, he was named editor of the *Christian Guardian*, a newspaper published by the Methodist Church. He was known for his attacks on the Church of England's exclusive claims to Clergy Reserves. While he initially leaned toward reform politics, in 1833 he came out in opposition to Mackenzie's radical views.

In 1841, he was appointed first principal of the University of Victoria College. From 1844 to 1876, he was chief superintendent of education for Canada West. During that time he established the *Journal of Education*, which he edited until his death in 1882.

SIMCOE, John Graves

John Graves Simcoe was born in England in 1752. He joined the British Army at the age of nineteen and was sent to America when the American Revolution broke out. He proved himself an able soldier, and was given command of the Queen's Rangers, a unit made-up of Loyalists. In 1781, he returned to England and became a Member of Parliament. In 1791, with the passage of the Constitutional Act, Simcoe was appointed the first lieutenant governor of Upper Canada.

Some of Simcoe's policies were very far-sighted. He tried to open the province by encouraging immigration and building roads. He served as lieutenant governor for four years, and then returned to England where he died in 1806.

STRACHAN, John

John Strachan was born in Scotland in 1778. He came to Canada in 1799 to tutor the children of wealthy merchants in Kingston. Later he established his own school in Cornwall and became a highly respected educator.

In 1804, Strachan was ordained a priest of the Church of England and appointed curate of Cornwall. He was transferred to York as rector in 1812 and became archdeacon of that city in 1825. In 1839, he was consecrated bishop of the newly created diocese of Toronto.

Strachan's central concerns were always religion and education, but he realized that to achieve his objectives he would have to take an active role in provincial politics. In 1815, he was appointed to the Executive Council and five years later to the Legislative Council. The Family Compact controlled the government of Upper Canada at that time and Strachan was a leading figure in that group. In keeping with the conservative views of the Compact, he upheld the right of the Church of England to the total benefits from clergy reserves.

Strachan remained an important and influential figure in the political, religious and educational life of Upper Canada almost until his death in 1867.

TALBOT, Thomas

Thomas Talbot was born in Ireland in 1771. He entered the British army in 1782, when he was only eleven years old. In 1790 he came to Canada. Two years later, he was appointed private secretary to Lieutenant Governor Simcoe. He served Simcoe until 1794, when he returned to England and became lieutenant-colonel in command of a foot regiment. After seeing some military action in Europe, he returned to Upper Canada. It was then that he received several thousand acres of land with which he hoped to found a settlement. He established his home at Port Talbot, on Lake Erie, and from there he governed his settlers for about fifty years.

From 1822 to 1832, he was a member of the Legislative Council of Upper Canada, but he took little real interest in politics. He died in 1853 with a reputation for having been a very eccentric man.

TRAILL, Catherine Parr

Born in London, England in 1802, Catherine Strickland married Lieutenant Thomas Traill in 1832. They had four sons and five daughters. Immediately after their marriage, they emigrated to Canada. For seven years, they pioneered near present-day Lakefield, Ontario and later lived in Peterborough and at Rice Lake. Mrs. Traill's strength of character and common sense enabled her to cope cheerfully and effectively with the hardships and isolation of pioneer life.

Like her sister, Susanna Moodie, Mrs. Traill had begun writing before her marriage. The most notable of her books, *The Backwoods of Canada*, is an accurate picture of pioneer life written to counteract the glowing descriptions put out by land companies anxious to attract immigrants. She was an ardent naturalist and wrote several books describing the plants of Upper Canada. She also published sketches, stories, and several novels for children.

Mrs. Traill lived a long life and spent her last years in Lakefield, Ontario where she died at the age of ninety-seven.

For Discussion

INTRODUCTION

1) Imagine that you are ordered to move tonight. You have about three hours to gather everything together but you only have the family car as a means of transportation. What will you take? What must be left behind?
2) Why is this situation similar to the experience of the early immigrants to Upper Canada?
3) What items would you value most if you were moving into the wilderness?

NEW SETTLERS CREATE A PROVINCE

1) How were the United Empire Loyalists different from the French Canadians?

The Assembly in Action — Politics and Rebellion
1) What is an Assembly?
2) Who was William Lyon Mackenzie?
3) Why was he discontented?
4) Did he accomplish anything?

Land Ownership in Upper Canada
1) What were the Clergy Reserves?
2) What were land grants?
3) What was a location ticket?
4) What is a speculator?
5) Why did land ownership create problems?

Indian Settlements
1) Who was Joseph Brant?
2) Who was John Deseronto?
3) Where did these Indian immigrants settle?

Loyalists and "Late Loyalists"
1) Who were the Loyalists?
2) Where did they settle?
3) What is a "late Loyalist?"

Successes and Failures
1) Why were some groups successful while others failed?
2) Explain how some settlers used a 'system.'
3) Who was William Berczy?
4) Who was Lord Selkirk?

New Settlers Come from Overseas
1) What kind of population did Upper Canada have in 1812?
2) How did this population change?
3) How did the British government assist immigration?

Leaders of Settlement
1) How did William Dickson promote settlement?
2) How did Colonel Talbot promote settlement?
3) How did the Canada Company promote settlement?
4) Which system of settlement is best in your opinion? Why?

A Cross-Section of Society
1) How did conditions differ for the wealthy?
2) How did the Strickland family contribute to Canadian history? (Consult the books of Catharine Traill and Susanna Moodie.)
3) Who are the Amish?
4) Where did Europeans settle in Upper Canada?

LIFE ON A PIONEER FARM

Starting a Farm
1) What is potash?
2) How did pioneers make use of their natural surroundings?
3) Can you find any evidence of these uses today?
4) Contrast the tools of pioneer farmers with modern farming machines.

The Problems Farmers Faced
1) Explain each of the following problems: long hours, helpers, isolation.

Visiting a Pioneer Home
1) Why were log houses unsatisfactory?
2) Describe the interior of a typical farm house.
3) Draw and label a floor plan for this pioneer home.
4) How did the pioneer home change as the family became wealthier?

Pioneer Food
1) Draw a daily menu for a pioneer farmer.
2) Which foods were expensive and therefore luxuries?

Household Tasks
1) Explain the many necessary household tasks (candle making, meat preservation, grain preparation, bread making, flax preparation).

The Family
1) What is a role?
2) What was the role of the male in pioneer life?
3) What was the role of the female in pioneer life?
4) What were the roles of the children?
5) How have these roles changed?

LIFE IN THE TOWNS AND CITIES

The Growth of Towns
1) Why did Kingston become an important town?
2) Why did Niagara become an important town?
3) Why did York become an important town?

Smaller Urban Centres
1) What businesses led to the growth of small towns?
2) Where were these towns located in all cases? Why?
3) How did these towns differ from modern towns?

THE GROWTH OF UPPER CANADA
1) How had Upper Canada changed by 1841?

Religion and Churches
1) How did the Christian churches contribute to life in Upper Canada?
2) What religious groups were common?
3) Is there any evidence of these groups in your community today?

The Churches and Social Problems
1) Why was alcohol a problem?
2) How did the churches try to control this problem?

Schools
1) Why were there few schools?
2) Contrast a typical common school with your own school. List the differences.

Health and Medical Care
1) Why was medical care poor?
2) Where did people get medical advice?
3) Where were babies born?

Upper Canada and the Future
1) How did the people of Upper Canada affect life in Ontario today?

Selected Further Reading

Abrahamson, Una. *God Bless our Home: Domestic Life in Nineteenth Century Canada*. Toronto: Burns & MacEachern, 1966. A guide to nineteenth century life.

The Canadians. Toronto: Fitzhenry & Whiteside. This series of brief biographies includes the lives of Elizabeth Simcoe, Egerton Ryerson, Joseph Brant, William Lyon Mackenzie, Susanna Moodie, and Laura Secord.

Cook, Lyn. *The Secret of Willow Castle*. Toronto: Macmillan, 1966. A girl from Napanee has a cousin by the name of John A. Macdonald.

Downie, Mary Alice and Downie, John. *Honour Bound*. Toronto: Oxford, 1971. A family of United Empire Loyalists settle in Kingston where the children discover a mystery.

Eaton, Sara. *Lady of the Backwoods: A Biography of Catherine Parr Traill*. Toronto: McClelland and Stewart, 1969. A fictionalized account of Mrs. Traill's life.

German, Tony. *Tom Penny*. Toronto: PMA Books, 1977. The tale of a boy's danger-filled journey from England to a new home in pioneer Upper Canada.

German, Tony. *River Race*. Toronto: PMA Books, 1979. Further adventures of Tom Penny in the lumber business of the Ottawa Valley.

Grayson, L.M. and Grayson, Paul. *Paddles and Wheels: Everyday Life and Travel in Canada*. Toronto: Oxford, 1974. Transportation in early Canada is presented through a readable text and good illustrations.

Guillet, Edwin C. *Pioneer Arts and Crafts*. Toronto: University of Toronto Press, 1968. Well-illustrated account of pioneer days and ways.

McKenzie, Ruth. *Laura Secord: the Legend and the Lady*. Toronto: McClelland and Stewart, 1971. A biography of one of Canada's famous heroines.

Minhinnick, Jeanne. *At Home in Upper Canada*. Toronto: Clarke, Irwin, 1970. A well-illustrated account of life in pioneer Ontario.

Moodie, Susanna. *Roughing it in the Bush.* Toronto: McClelland and Stewart, 1962. Older readers will enjoy an English gentlewoman's account of the rough Canadians and their unyielding land.

Neering, R. and Garrod, S. *Life of the Loyalists*. Toronto: Fitzhenry and Whiteside, 1975. An excellent and well-illustrated description of pioneer days.

Reaney, James. *The boy with an Я in his hand*. Toronto: Macmillan, 1965. A novel set in the years just before the 1837 Rebellion.

Traill, Catherine Parr. *The Backwoods of Canada*. Toronto: McClelland and Stewart, 1966. An honest picture of pioneer life in the form of letters from Mrs. Traill to her mother.

Index

Amish, 41

Baldoon Settlement, 30–31
Berczy, William, 30
Berlin, U.C., 41
Bobcaygeon, U.C., 41, 66
Brant, Joseph, 22; biography, 88; illus., 22
By, Colonel John, 67
Bytown, U.C. 67; illus., 68

Canada Company, 15, 19, 38–40
Candlemaking, 51–52, 55; illus., 52
Church of England, 15, 18, 78–81
Clergy Reserves, 18–19, 78, 79
Cloth and clothing, 56–57
Conestoga Wagons, 29; illus., 28
Conservatives, 14–15
Constitutional Act, 1791, 13, 18
Crown Reserves, 18–19

Deseronto, John, 22
Dickson, William, 36
Durham, Lord, 17; biography, 88; *Report*, 17
Dunlop, William "Tiger", 38; biography, 88

Education, 57–58, 82–85
Executive Council, 13–18

Family Compact, 15, 17, 78
Food, pioneer, 52–55
French Canadians, 12–13, 21
Furniture, 46, 50–51

Galt, John, 38
Galt, U.C., 36
Goderich, U.C., 40
Guelph, U.C., 40; illus., 66

Houses, 48–50, 72–73

Immigrants
    American, 27–33
    British, 28–33, 40
    French, 30
    German, 30, 41
    Irish, 33
    Scot, 27–29
Indians, 21–24

Kingston, U.C., 60–62, 74; illus., 61

Late Loyalists, 27
Legislative Assembly, 13–18
Legislative Council, 13–18

Location tickets, 20
London, U.C., 63, 66

Mackenzie, William Lyon, 15–17; biography, 89; illus., 17
Markham, U.C., 30
Medical care, 85–87
Methodists, 28, 77–78, 80–81
Moodie, Susanna, 40, 54; biography, 89
Moravian Indians, 22–24

Niagara, U.C., 62–63, 74

Perth, U.C., 30
Peterborough, U.C., 34, 67
Population of Upper Canada, 32

Rebellion of 1837, 17
Reformers, 14–15, 27, 78
Responsible government, 17-18
Robinson, Peter, 33–34; biography, 89
Ryerson, Egerton, 80

Schools, 80–81, 82–85; illus., 83
Seigniorial system, 13
Selkirk, Lord, 30–31
Shade, Absalom, 36
Simcoe, John Graves, 21, 26, 62, biography, 90; illus., 14
Six Nations Indians, 21–24
Slavery, 21
Speculators, 20
Strachan, John, 15, 78, 81, 83, 84; biography, 90; illus., 80
Stratford, U.C., 40
Strickland, Samuel, 40

Talbot, Thomas, 36–38; biography, 91; illus., 36
Temperance movement, 82
Tools, farm, 45–46
Toronto, 63–64, 69, 72; illus., 64
Traill, Catherine Parr, 40; biography, 91
Transportation, 46–47, 74
    roads, 37, 62–63, 68–69
    water routes, 60–62, 64–65, 67

Union Act, 1841, 13, 20, 87
United Empire Loyalists, 9, 13, 24–26

War of 1812, 19, 24, 27, 33

York *See* Toronto